Terayama Shūji

The Crimson Thread
of Abandon

Stories

Terayama Shūji

The Crimson Thread of Abandon

Stories

Translated with an Introduction
by Elizabeth L. Armstrong

MerwinAsia
Portland, Maine

MERWIN

A S I A

Distributed by the University of Hawai'i Press

Library of Congress Control Number: 2014940127

ISBN 978-1-937385-49-1 (paperback)

ISBN 978-1-937385-50-7 (hardcover)

Printed in the United States of America

The paper used in this publication meets the minimum requirements
of the American National Standard for Information Services—
Permanence of Paper for Printed Library Materials,
ANSI/NISO Z39/48-1992

Book and cover design:
Lucian Burg, Lu Design Studios, Portland, Maine

Contents

Contents

ACKNOWLEDGMENTS

I wish to express my deep gratitude to the many people who have given me the benefit of their support, wisdom and expertise. I thank Mitsuru and Kurumi Hiki for their unflagging energy and willingness to work through my translations with me. I would not have been able to complete this work without their frank and apposite explanations. In addition, there are several generations of teaching assistants who have given me their candid input, which in turn improved the translation. George Casper, a technical magician, also has my eternal gratitude.

I wish to thank Terayama Eiko for granting me permission to translate these stories, and in particular, I thank Shiraishi Sei for being an invaluable liaison in the process. I am also grateful to Professor Sarah Strong for urging me to pursue publication of these stories. I will always be nourished and fortified by her advice and encouragement.

I thank my husband, Erik Lofgren, for his unstinting support and for generously sharing his perspective on my work. I thank my children, Rebekah and Mariah Lofgren, as well for reading my translations and providing insightful comments.

Finally, I thank my mother and father, James and Carol Armstrong, who instilled in me a delight in words, and a deep-seated conviction that storytelling is seminal in how human beings understand, translate and sustain themselves.

Elizabeth L. Armstrong

INTRODUCTION

I first encountered Terayama Shūji's writing in a most unlikely spot. While I was waiting in the Iwakura Public Library in northern Kyoto for my deeply engrossed four-year old daughter to finish looking at a picture book, I was leafing through a variety of short story collections for my own entertainment. For a number of years, I had been looking for stories of appropriate length and content to use as texts in my advanced Japanese language class. One slim paperback came to hand entitled, 赤糸で縫いとじられた物語, literally, "Tales sewn up with a red thread" and I began reading. The length of the stories seemed manageable as class materials, which was the first important criterion of acceptability. Upon an initial cursory read, I discovered also that the stories themselves were challenging and magnetically engaging.

The stories are described as "tales for adults", and indeed they are written in such a way as to mimic and sometimes parody classic fairy tale style. Yet, these tales are far from traditional in content; rather, they turn our conventional thinking and expectations upside down. There are instances in which we are presented with young men who are not noble and dashing, barons who crave counterfeit rather than authentic treasure, a knavish seeker in a game of hide-and-seek, and lovers who work at cross purposes rather than living happily ever after. Buffoons are validated and noble characters are undermined. This topsy-turvy world of Terayama is unsettling and disconcerting at times, but his world is, without a doubt, thought provoking. As I stood in the Iwakura Library I knew I had found not only teaching materials but also literature that I wanted to share with an English-speaking readership.

Terayama Shūji (1935–1983) was one of the most prolific "outlaw" writers in the 1960s and '70s in Japan. He produced an enormous body of work in multiple genres ranging from poetry, essays and novels to short stories, film scripts, and plays. The sheer volume and often provocative nature of his work accounts in large measure for his renown, but despite his notoriety domestically, he remains virtually unknown outside Japan. Even within the world of letters in Japan he was branded as an iconoclast and agitator, frequently relegated to the fringes of even those among the literati expressing counter-culture, revolutionary ideas about social behavior, sexuality, and philosophy.

Terayama was born in Aomori Prefecture in northern Japan where he lived with his parents until his father was conscripted to fight in World War II. His father subsequently died in Indonesia when Terayama was nine-years old. In the immediate postwar turmoil, Terayama's mother left him in the care of an uncle to go work on an American military base on the southern island of Kyushu. Kozue Uzawa, who has translated many of Terayama's poems, writes, "His complex feelings of being abandoned by his mother, longing for his dead father and siblings he did not have, and longing to be freed from reality are expressed with extraordinary imagination."[1]

It is precisely this deep preoccupation with abandonment

1. http://simplyhaiku.com/SHv6n3/reviews/Terayama.html

and thwarted pursuit of love and attachment which is the primary leitmotif in his collection of "tales for adults"(おとなの童話 otona no dōwa). The first section of this translation comprises the tales which were published in 2000 under the title 赤糸で縫いとじられた物語 (Akaito de nuitojirareta monogatari), which I have rendered as *The Crimson Thread of Abandon*. The second section holds a complement of tales which appear in his collected works. The crimson thread noted in the title aptly describes the nature of the stories and the interstitial webbing that links one to another. These stories are joined together thematically by the metaphorical twisting together of unrequited love, abandonment, irremediable separation, and disappointment. Told in the manner of fantasy and magic realism, the stories are populated with characters who face the vagaries of fortune which keep happiness always just out of their reach. The stories are disturbing, melancholy, and poignant in turn, for he insists upon a lack of closure and intentionally withholds the possibility of happy resolution. He is a realist speaking through the medium of fantasy.

Fairy tales are generally considered to be mythological or folkloric narrative which convey either a didactic tale or transmits cultural memes to youth. Terayama employs the construct of the fairy tale, but he directs the narrative, sometimes rough and gruesome, to an adult audience, much as the Grimm Brothers did in their original and unexpurgated version of *Grimms' Fairy Tales* (1812). The brothers Grimm collected their stories for cultural posterity; Terayama creates his tales using narrative metaphor to process and reveal perverse ironies in life. For Terayama, fairy tales are there to be interpreted and reinterpreted as one sees fit. His own personal interpretation of the traditional tale "The Emperor's

New Clothes" is novel at best, and most certainly unique. He writes:

> I love the figure of the emperor in Hans Christian Anderson's "The Emperor's New Clothes." I am convinced that he knew he was naked and he just wanted to stun the population. This emperor was hyper-conscious of fashion, so he was quick to discern new trends as well as the hearts of men. Surely he had read Machiavelli's *Il Principe* and determined that his policy would be to become an adored leader rather than one that was feared. To become an adored leader, it is necessary to bungle benignly on occasion. That said, the leader of a country must manage somehow not to bungle politically . . . He cherished peace over war and was more interested in how well he was dressed for meetings or hunting parties.

> But this was a manifestation of his painstaking efforts to become an un-emperor-like emperor. He rebelled against the concept of an emperor who sported a crown and beard, and adorned himself with stately medals in the image of the King of Hearts. The emperor repeated habitually, "I don't want to become a symbol."

He goes on to describe the two tailors.

> Who were these dissemblers who came to this country selling the most beautiful clothes in the world? One theory has it that they were spies from another country. They attempted to get as close as possible to the emperor for as long as possible, by assuming the role of tailors, so they could report back intelligence on his activities. Another scenario maintains that they simply wanted to turn a quick profit and had no ulterior motive at all. But one must not ignore the theory that these men were religious

men or poets. In order to enlighten them about "God" and "Beauty" as intangible entities derived from abstract concepts, the tailors presented a mock Socratic proposition which caused the emperor and his subjects some consternation... There are many things in our midst which are invisible but have value. If one said that something is worthless if it is invisible, then culture would be reduced to ashes.[2]

Given Terayama's unconventional interpretation of this classic tale, it is not surprising to find that his own fairy tales might also reflect this kind of nonconformist posture.

In this volume, the beginning of each tale presents a seemingly quotidian circumstance, into which Terayama then proceeds to introduce the improbable or impossible with no apology or hint of incongruity. "The Eraser" depicts a sailor who comes by a magic eraser that can erase things and people, while in "Memory Shots" a doctor injects his patients with memories donated to a memory bank. "Bird in a Bottle" has people morphing into birds at will, and the protagonist of "Yesterday" takes photographs which show how the subjects will look ten years in the future. There are poignant tales like "One-Centimeter Journey" which is reminiscent of O'Henry's "Gift of the Magi." "Gotta Dance" is reminiscent of the ballet "The Red Shoes," and "Ribbon of the Sea" which tells of a yellow ribbon migrating its evil misfortunes from one person to another, leaving misery in its wake. There are even

2. Terayama Shūji 寺山修司, "Anderusen no 'hadaka no osama' wa sugoi nikutaibi datta" アンデルセンの「はだかの王さま」はすごい肉体美だった in Vol. 4 of "Terayama Shūji Chosakushū" 寺山修司著作集), ed. Yamada Masao 山田昌男 and Shiraishi Sei 白石征 (Tokyo: Quintessence Publishing Co. Ltd., 2009) pp. 189-190.

instances in which Terayama teases the reader into imagining he is making a Western classical reference. In "Lena's Death," Lena the swan is tantalizingly reminiscent of the episode in Greek mythology of Leda and the Swan, a story of rape most famously depicted in W.B. Yeat's poem of the same name. Zeus, disguised as a swan, rapes Leda, the daughter of an Aetolian king and wife of the king of Sparta. Terayama's story changes the woman's name slightly and gives her the role of swan, isolated, destitute, and despondent. Through Terayama's personal version of jumbled pastiche, we are invited to imagine abandoned Leda and her fate from a completely different perspective.

Terayama's prose is straightforward in the original, and I have tried to maintain that plain forthrightness in English, which at times can appear almost too concise. The spareness of his prose is compensated amply, however, by the depth of his love of word play and abundant literary references which can sometimes be authentic and sometime parodic. Translation of word play is arguably the most formidable challenge a translator might encounter. There are instances when the text virtually brims with Japanese puns, double entendre, obscure references, and onomatopoetic euphony. Terayama is not shy about making copious references to Japanese and Western literature and literary figures which range from the well-known to the arcane. He may invoke Buddhist teachings one minute only to mention cursorily such obscure characters as Dr. Mabuse, created by the French writer Norbert Jacques, or in passing, invoke the name of the humorist Pierre Henri Cami. Where possible, I have rendered the Japanese into the crucible of English and let it take its own form and effect. When the

Japanese and English do not coincide with equivalent effect, I have offered footnotes to elucidate the text.

Although fairy tales are often told from the perspective of an omniscient narrator, Terayama will, without compunction, modulate from omniscient narrator, to first person narrator, to the use of his own voice as the author speaking directly to the reader. Further, the prose of many stories is often interspersed with poems which behave frequently as a savant narrator who willfully interjects, changing the pace of the narrative or adumbrating a subsequent development.

Another aspect of the connective "red thread" in this collection is manifest in Terayama's use of a cast of recurring stock characters, using such names as Alice, or Johnny or Mizue, repeatedly. Characters who have appeared in one story may reappear in a completely different situation with a different personality. Alice, might be the main character of one story, but make a cameo appearance in another. Over and over again, we see sailors, caskets, the game of hide and seek, and a madam. These and others are the cast he chooses to convey stories that could be the stuff of nightmares, emotional confusion, and chaos.

Finally, these tales for an adult audience are never afforded a happy ending, or more accurately, are never given a fully completed ending, one to which Western readers may be accustomed. Terayama insists on withholding a happy resolution for any of these stories, and yet though he speaks the language of abandonment and disconnection, the reader, ultimately, is not abandoned by Terayama in a wasteland of despair. He seeks desperately to connect with the reader through the momentum he generates as he propels the characters forward, making each one suffer, often abandoning them before they have a chance to grow, reflect and take heart once again. It is precisely this momentum with which Terayama engages the reader on a psychological and emotional level. Terayama is a realist for whom the search for fulfillment is futile because the wholeness he seeks is unattainable. He depicts this reality through fantasy, thus distancing himself and the reader from inevitable misfortune. The brilliance of these intimate tales of "incompleteness" lies in the mote of something familiar that jogs our own memories, and reminds us of our own search for wholeness.

Terayama Shūji

The Crimson Thread
of Abandon

Stories

Ribbon of the Sea

She tied the ribbon in a bow.
She tied the ribbon in a bow.
The beautiful girl can never go home.

One

The old woman with the big wart, who appeared in the picture book, irked Mizue no end. So she decided to take a pair of scissors to her and cut her right out of the page. That night, when the moon hung in the sky like a well-washed plate, Mizue opened up the book on her bed and set about cutting out the old woman. Suddenly, the old woman, liberated from the book, spoke up.

"What a relief! I was sick and tired of living on that same page for so long." The old woman muscled her way up onto the lap of an astonished Mizue.

"No need to worry, dear. I won't be here long. I've decided to go right back home to where Batty the Umbrella and Cleft-palate Goosey are waiting for me. But, since you have been good enough to set me free, I'll do you the favor of giving you some valuable advice.

"Beware the ribbon. Beware the yellow ribbon, for it will bring nothing but misfortune." Mizue did not really understand. She thought to ask what the old woman was

1

talking about, but the wind gusted all of a sudden. Freed from the page, the paper cutout of the old woman was so light that the wind simply blew her out of sight in the twinkling of an eye.

Mizue was quite taken aback. Then she heaved a great sigh as she looked back at the picture book and the empty space where the old woman had been.

"Beware the ribbon. Beware the yellow ribbon, for it will bring nothing but misfortune." She imagined that this warning was all in jest. Yet, it also sounded like a foreboding incantation. The more she thought about it, the more confused she became, so Mizue thought it best to forget all about it. You see, Mizue was a little girl, only seven-years old.

Two

> Seven girls with ribbons
> fell into a well seven times.
> The ribbons fell fluttering down.
> Sorrowful ribbons fell fluttering down.

Mizue received an alarm clock as a gift on her tenth birthday. It was in a cardboard box tied up with a yellow ribbon. Mizue liked the ribbon even better than the clock, so she tied up her hair with it.

She looked in the mirror and asked, "How do I look?" To which the mirror answered, "It suits you beautifully." So Mizue, with the yellow ribbon fluttering in the wind, went to show it to Mr. Longhand at the flour mill.

Mr. Longhand was Mizue's only "friend," who was forever telling her fascinating stories. He had told her stories like

"Canning Just About Everything" and "The Pencil That Wouldn't Stop Writing."

Yet, when Mizue reached the flour mill the door was shut tight and Mr. Longhand was nowhere to be seen. She knocked, and then heard a voice from inside.

"Who is it?"

"It's me," called out Mizue. "I've brought something lovely to show you." She heard Mr. Longhand clear his throat. "This is not a good time," he said. "Come back later." Mizue was sadly disappointed. "I don't want to come back later! I want to come in now!"

But Mr. Longhand repeated himself, "This is not a good time. Come back later." Once, Mizue had seen Mr. Longhand and the maid Marie entangled naked together, covered in flour. She thought for a moment that he was up to no good again.

Suddenly, she was overcome by the desire to do something wicked. I'll just shove the door open and surprise him. He'll apologize, I'll show him my ribbon and he'll tell me how pretty it is, she thought. Overpowered by the thought of this naughty deed, she threw open the door.

Whoosh!

Out came a blast of the flour mill's exhaust. Like a great gust of wind, the white flour was blown up in the air and hit Mizue squarely in the face. Before she could call for help, flour struck her in both eyes, and she was blinded.

Poor Mizue of the Yellow Ribbon was blind from then on. It was only after she lost her sight that she recalled the warning from the old woman. "Beware the yellow ribbon, for it will bring nothing but misfortune." Mizue was the first victim.

Three

> A ribbon in the bridegroom's teeth,
> a ribbon blindfolding a little girl,
> a ribbon transformed into a butterfly,
> a green ribbon that never sold,
> a ribbon named Misfortune.
> Which ribbon is the longest?

Mizue's discarded yellow ribbon lay in the grass on the side of the road for some time. There a mother thrush flew down and took it up in her beak. She was going to use it as decoration for her nest, which was filled with seven newly hatched chicks.

However, the thrush, holding the yellow ribbon in her beak, became a bright target for Don the Hunter. Don the Hunter raised his gun and with one shot the thrush was done.[1] Sadly enough, the thrush had not known that the ribbon she had plucked up was the yellow ribbon of misfortune.

Four

Don the Hunter thought it odd that the thrush he shot was holding a yellow ribbon. Yet, when he took it in his hand it fluttered so beautifully in the wind that he decided to bring it home for his daughter Saki. Saki was Don's seventeen-year old daughter who was wild-looking and very beautiful. Lamentably, however, she was mute. Don loved his daughter and wanted to do whatever he could to give her the power of speech. So he took her to enchanters and magicians, engaged detectives to find her lost language, used an air pump to give

---

1. *Don* is the sound of a gunshot in Japanese, which is homophonous with the hunter's name.

her a mass infusion of words, and took her to Dr. Mabuse[2] for vocalization lessons.

When he discovered that she could speak in her dreams, but not in reality, he considered giving her an operation which would switch dreams for reality. He also had prayers said over her for a thousand Arabian nights.

At long last, he finally obtained the once-in-a-lifetime opportunity for Saki to speak just three times. On the evening they learned of this, father and daughter embraced and wept together. Saki, overwhelmed with joy, burst out, "Oh Father, thank you!"

Don, looked at her in astonishment which turned to consternation, "Idiot!" he shouted. "How could you waste one of the only three chances you have at a moment like this?!"

Saki was rocked back by her father's fierceness, and blurted out without thinking, "Oh Father, I'm sorry!"

So she had used up two of the three chances she had to speak, leaving only one remaining. The two conferred and decided that she would use her final opportunity to speak to say "I love you" when she opened her heart to a person she truly loved. Until that day came, she vowed never to say another word.

It was around that time when Saki encountered someone she felt strongly about. He was a violinist with a limp, who came to the mountain each day to practice his violin. Saki could feel herself strongly drawn to him as she watched him from afar. It was almost as if she were attracted to him by the force of fate.

One day, Saki gave the violinist one mountain lily.

2. Dr. Mabuse is a fictional character created by the French writer Norbert Jacques in his novel *Dr. Mabuse, der Spieler*.

The next day, the violinist played a song he had composed especially for Saki about the mountain lily. Saki made up her mind that tomorrow she would use the last chance she had in reserve to speak for this occasion.

It was at this juncture that Don came home with the yellow ribbon. He was in a jovial mood. "Isn't this ribbon pretty? It would certainly look pretty in your hair," he said. Tomorrow was to be the momentous day when she would use her once-in-a-lifetime chance to speak, so naturally she wanted to dress up a bit. She gladly received the yellow ribbon and tied it up in her hair.

"You look just lovely, dear," said Don.

There was no mirror in this mountain cottage, for Don was a poor man and had no need for such things. So Saki, wanting to see how she looked adorned with the yellow ribbon, set out for the river in the ravine behind their home and looked at her reflection in the water. It was the first time she had taken a really good look at herself since she had become a mature woman. The yellow ribbon in her long, black hair looked almost like a flower in bloom. Bedazzled by her own beauty, she sighed and whispered, "How lovely I am." When she suddenly realized what she had done, it was too late. She had spoken for the last time in her life, and was devastated that she would never be able to share her true feelings with the violinist.

The very day before she was to speak the words "I love you", Saki had squandered the chance she had long awaited. She was desolate. Her life seemed meaningless. There she was, all alone, her figure reflected in the ravine's river. She closed her eyes and listened to the song of the kingfisher. Then, with the yellow ribbon still tied in her hair, Saki leapt into the torrent.

Five

When Saki's body was found, the yellow ribbon was nowhere to be seen. It most likely came untied and floated out into the broad expanse of ocean. But I can no longer take it upon myself to write about who will be the next person to pick up that ribbon and suffer the misfortune it brings. My pen has declared that it will no longer write tales of woe and unhappiness.

Still, misfortune will not vanish from the world as long as the yellow ribbon remains floating somewhere at sea. One can only take solace in imagining the yellow ribbon being carried farther and farther away from shore.

> He tied a ribbon in a bow.
> He tied a ribbon in a bow.
> The beautiful sailor
> has lost his safe harbor.

No one can write a sequel to this story. This is because I have sealed it up in a cardboard box and thrown it out to sea with all the rest of the troubles in this world. Perhaps the sequel and the yellow ribbon will encounter each other at sea on a moonlit night. So, farewell. If you chance upon a cardboard box tied up with a yellow ribbon on a seafaring voyage, do not pick it up. If you do, the sequel to this story will begin.

"A tear is the smallest ocean in the world . . ."

BIRD IN A BOTTLE

A riddle, a riddle.
What bird cannot flee the flock?
The bird that is alone (a loon).[1]

One

"What a strange bird," thought the boy. The bird was reading the newspaper. He experienced a weird sensation as he watched the bird peck at each individual character in the stock market column of *The Times* spread out on the table, as if they were grains of rice. It was the bird that had flitted in through an open window one day and taken up residence in the boy's bedroom, but the boy had no idea what kind of bird it was or where it came from.

The bird evinced a rather supercilious air. Bird though it was, it would do things like clear its throat haughtily, surreptitiously open one of his father's whiskey bottles and secretly help himself; and it would light on his father's pipe and begin to clean it with his beak.

"It's almost as if . . . ", thought the boy, "I'm watching someone's father."

---

1. なぞなぞ　たてろ。同じ鳥でも飛ばないとりはなあんだ？それはひとり、という鳥だ。Literally, pose a riddle, a riddle. What "tori" (bird) cannot fly even though it is a bird? It is the bird that is "hitori" (solitary, alone, one person, not a bird) by itself.

Around that time, a woman, weeping bitterly, came into the private eye's office, daubing her tears with a handkerchief. The private eye, whose mustache looked much like a black butterfly, leaned forward with his elbows on the police report and said, "So, in other words . . .

"It was your husband who disappeared, right?" The woman nodded silently.

"Your husband, who never missed a day of work in thirty years at the Weather Bureau Observatory, just up and disappeared one day. And you don't have the remotest idea where he went or why he vanished. Is that right?"

"Yes, that's right," answered the woman. "If it was something I did, I'll fix it. If he has found someone else, I'll deal with it. I need him to just come home even if only for a moment. It is too much to bear that he left without a word."

"All right," announced the mustached private eye. "I'll find him for you somehow."

The private eye, however, could not have begun to imagine that the man who disappeared had turned into a bird.

Two

Then a series of strange events occurred. A taxi driver picked up a family of three in front of a bar, but only two got out at their destination. They were tipsy and bid farewell to the driver with a drunk's usual line, "Hey buddy, tanks a lot!" as they disappeared into the darkness.

"That's strange. I could have sworn I picked up three people," he thought. The driver proceeded to look into the back seat and caught his breath; for there was a bird, drunk, sleeping peacefully without a care in the world.

Three

It was music class for the children at school. The students were to sing the lyrics the teacher had written on the blackboard.

"Everyone sing out, now. Ready? One, two, three . . ."

> Vanish, the old lady,
> vanish, the train I ride.
> Vanish, my hometown,
> good-bye, good-bye.
> I waved, and out of the blue
> came the moon.

The children were singing with all their might, when all of a sudden the teacher, at the front of the classroom, began to cough violently. His head went down on the desk, shoulders shaking, and he began to shrink.

> "Vanish", the name on a dusty bottle on
> a back shelf in the liquor store.
> Peering in the dark darkness
> I suddenly encountered a bird.

Suddenly, the teacher hugged himself and squatted down. When he raised his head, he had been transformed to something no larger than a fist. Upon further inspection, he had suede wings protruding from his shoulders. With two or three strong flaps he sailed out the classroom window.

"Hey!" shouted one child. "The teacher just winged out!"

Four

This phenomenon continued to occur. No one knew, however, how much of the witnesses' testimony to believe. Lie detectors don't work on birds, and there was no scientific basis for what the witnesses reported.

A prostitute downtown said, "In bed, he was a sailor. The man had a blue butterfly tattoo he got at a tattoo shop in Madrid. He was hairy and pushy, and wore me out. But when it was time for him to pay, he suddenly disappeared and there was this bird on the bed. Damn it, I told him, I'm not about to get stiffed my money just because you've heard the rumors, and are trying to pull one over on me by pretending to be a bird. I looked under the bed and all over for him, but I couldn't find that sailor anywhere."

The chicken shish kabob man said, "There I was, plucking the birds for the shish kabob, when I noticed that one of the birds was acting strangely. It seemed to be talking to someone intently. I pretended not to notice but listened carefully. I couldn't really understand what it was saying, but it was something about two hemispheres, Hindu history, planets, and such. So, I asked, 'What the heck are you?' and the bird had the nerve to say 'I'm an astronomer.' And he went on to say that he was preparing a manuscript for the paper he was to deliver at a conference on Saturday about the role of Venus in classical astronomy. After a bit, I plucked him and he joined the others as shish kabob."

The elevator girl said, "No doubt about it, when I closed the door there were nine girls in school uniforms. But when I opened the door, nine birds flew out. No, I didn't stop on the way from the first floor to the top floor, because my elevator was the non-stop."

The police officer said, "I was in a fix because no one believed me when I brought it in and told them this was the perpetrator. Yes, there is no denying there are more people bringing in real birds and trying to pin the blame on them, but the guy I brought in really was the perp.

"And after all this, my boss looked at me sourly and said, 'Accusing a bird isn't going to get you anywhere.' He wouldn't even give the okay for an investigation."

A child said, "My mom turned into a bird, and so I was playing with that bird . . . and then another bird came flying over and then there were two of 'em. I lost track of which one was Mommy, and when I was trying to figure that out, I heard a rifle shot and one bird dropped dead. I didn't know if Mommy was dead, or if Mommy was the one who was frightened off, so I can't figure out if I should cry or not."

Five

The population of birds grew as the population of people decreased in this town. The Sociology professor, who did research on what type of people were more prone to becoming birds, turned into a bird; and the linguist, who conducted an analysis of bird communication in hopes of solving the mystery, and contrived a language so he could "converse with the birds", also turned into a bird.

In short, bird transformation spread like a contagious disease without any clues as to how to stop it. There were even women who, by mistake, took a real bird aside and chastised him for changing his mind about her. There were those who lost their way chasing an unknown bird to a foreign country and never returned. And, there were pitiful old people who just kept eating bird food in hopes that they would turn into one.

The book entitled, *You Too Can Become a Bird* and the book *The Trick to Not Becoming a Bird* sold exactly the same number of copies. The sky, as usual, was gloomy and overcast.

Six

This is another one of those sad stories. The boy's name was Mugi. The girl's name was Saki. They loved each other and were soon to be married. Every Saturday night the two of them went out to a wheat field close to the airport and talked about the future as they watched the night flights.

One night, Mugi told the north New Guinean tale of "The God of Two Wishes."

"The God of Two Wishes is a deity which grants only two wishes before it succumbs to death."

"Only two?" asked Saki.

"Only two."

Saki had never seen The God of Two Wishes, but imagined what the god might be like. If the god could only grant two requests, what would she wish for? An azure sky, babies, a home, happiness for her and Mugi?

Then, one Saturday night, Saki went to their spot in the wheat field as she always did, but Mugi was nowhere to be seen. There was only one bird perched on a tree branch overhead.

"I guess Mugi is late tonight," she thought.

She waited late into the evening, but Mugi did not appear. Then, when the bird flew down and snuggled familiarly into her lap, she suddenly realized that her love had turned into a bird. Saki felt warm tears well up as she gazed at the singular bird she held in her hand.

A riddle, a riddle.
What bird cannot flee the flock?
The bird that is alone (a loon).

Sitting in the wheat field that night dozing with the bird held close to her cheek, Saki saw an apparition, the God of Two Wishes. On a sudden impulse, she made a wish.

"God of Two Wishes, please make me a bird, too."

There was a gust of wind. The bird in Saki's hand opened its eyes wide with desperation and worked its beak as if it had something pressing to say. In the whirl of the wind, Mugi rose with a mighty beat of his wings and became himself again just as Saki turned into a bird. Saki had asked to become a bird to be with Mugi, and Mugi had wished to become human again.

Mugi looked down at the sad little bird crouched next to him and said, "Alas! We've sacrificed ourselves, each for the other."

Sadly, neither Mugi nor Saki could transform again. The God of Two Wishes could not accommodate more than the two it had already granted. Mugi resigned himself never to marry, and made his life with his desolate little bird. Here ends the loon-ly story of a lonely anti-bird.

Yesterday

Again the cockrobin!
I thought I had killed it.

One

No one knew that Johnny had learned how to talk to the bird. All the residents of the island just smiled when they saw Johnny, dressed in shorts, walking along with a robin on his shoulder. Johnny was seventeen, lanky and tall. He took large strides with deer-like poise, and had the appearance of a boxer so deeply tanned that he could very well have been of mixed blood.

Two

Even Johnny himself couldn't figure out why he had acquired the ability to talk to the bird. He wasn't sure whether he spoke in bird language, or if the robin spoke in human language; or if neither were the case, and it was a special language unto itself instead. Occasionally he would try to observe himself objectively when talking with the bird, but somehow he would get so involved each time that he would forget to focus. He was certain, however, of two things: that he and the robin conducted real conversations, and that he and the bird considered each other their most trusted confidents. Johnny named the robin Words, and thus this is the story of Johnny and Words.

Three

There were many books in the collection of the island's library. Among the language-related titles alone, the shelves were filled with dictionaries for the languages of indigenous peoples in locations like Tibet and Madagascar; there were canine dictionaries as well. There were others like *Concise Cat Language*, *The Companion to Mirror Ideography Deciphering*, *The Encyclopedia of Lunar Communication*, *Dictionary of Creative Celestialese*, *Comprehensive Dictionary of Invisible Entities*, *A Random Collection of Alice's Insults and Verbal Abuse*, *Dictionary of Antelopese* (Revised Edition), *Conversations of the Dead: A Beginner's Guide to Verbatim Translation*, *The Complete Curse Companion*, *Hyena: A Three-week Self-study Language Course*, *Dictionary of Elementary Fetal Language*, and *Famous Quotes from Humpty-Dumpty*.

Yet, even among all these, for whatever reason, there was not one book about bird language. So it was Johnny who was the only person on the island (on earth, actually) who could talk to the bird.

Four

"In bird words," said the robin, "arms are called human branches. Shoulders are perches and legs are called moving roots." Johnny began to laugh. "So in human language that would make birds airplanes we can't fly in."

"In bird words, an airplane is the biggest bird there is," retorted the robin. "We call a tree, a guy; a lumberjack, an executioner. A birdcage is a concentration camp. Someone's messy hair is known as a boarding house dive. We write letters on leaves and the wind serves as our mail carrier."

"Fascinating," said Johnny. "I suppose a bird who sings beautifully is known as a chanteur."

"Yes, yes. Older birds warble like opera singers, but young ones sing any way they want. They sway on tree branches and sing to their heart's content. You won't find skylarks just trilling along anymore."

Five

Johnny had a girlfriend then. She was the daughter of the Consul General, and her name was Sephra. With blond shoulder-length hair, Sephra had an air of archaic properness. She would often read Brontë novels with a basket full of flowers on one arm, or paint pictures, or make the automaton play the Serenade for Left Hand; or she might spend the whole day mugging in front of the mirror as she searched for the entrance to Wonderland.

Sephra once sang Johnny the shortest song in the world which began with "lo-" and ended with "-ve."[1] She sang it a cappella. There was nothing in between "lo" and "ve," so it sounded rather like low-vee if you drew out the vowels a little. But since it was supposed to be the shortest song in the world, she sang it all in one breath, "love." She sang it for Johnny three times and he fell in love with her.

Johnny and Sephra liked to spend the entire day in the Consulate garden leaning on the white walls covered by tropical vines talking about everything and nothing.

They would discuss, for instance, whether the swirl of a

---

1. The syllables in Japanese are "a" (あ) and "i"(い), which in succession form the word "ai" (愛), or "love."

snail's shell winds left or right, if six-pointed stars exist, if it is better to open your right or left eye when kissing if you were to open your eyes at all. They liked to talk about where the most remote location in the world is, how to retrieve something you left in a dream by mistake, and how many different words there are in the world for "love."

While these two were talking, Words the robin, sat on Johnny's shoulder happily, sometimes nodding in agreement.

Six

"So, what do you think of Sephra?"

"She is cute enough," replied Words.

"Would you want her as your girlfriend if you weren't a robin?"

Words thought for a moment and then said, "She is cute, but . . . I wouldn't go that far."

"Really?! How come?" asked Johnny.

"She is a little too innocent for my tastes. I fancy a more mature woman; a bird who can really soar high in the sky."

"You're pretty cheeky for a robin," said Johnny, laughing. However, he didn't truly understand what Words was getting at. Words had wanted to say, "Sephra is not bad, but I like you much better than her, Johnny; and I don't want anyone to take you away from me."

Seven

A young man, a young woman, and a robin—this trio got quite a reputation on the island for being so close. They had rambling conversations in sunny glades or on the lawn of the Consulate garden. They talked about the fact that Marmalade, the cat, had eyebrows, about the Hatter's twins[2] who would even pee the same distance, about the fact that the most precise isosceles triangle on the island was the Consulate Secretary's nose, about the romance between Dormouse and Smoky Mouse, about the map of Treasure Island that seven-year old Carroll[3] knit at the caucus race without even knowing it. Every so often, Sephra would compose a song and sing it to Johnny.

> I wrote a smoky love letter
> with a smoky pen
> on some smoky paper.
> It vanished before you read it.

Eight

Unfortunately, tales of happiness don't continue for very long. Not a year had passed, when Sephra had to give Johnny some sad news.

"Johnny, . . ." she said, taking a rather formal tone, "we are going to have to leave this island."

"What?!" said Johnny alarmed (in the meantime, Words had blinked a hundred times).

"Why?!"

"The Consulate on this island is going to be shut down. My whole family is going to move to a neighboring island," replied Sephra.

Johnny shook his head in disbelief.

"So you are going to go and leave us here?"

"I have no choice," said Sephra. "I don't want to go, but it's all been decided for me."

---

2. Reference to the Mad Hatter in Alice in Wonderland.
3. Lewis Carroll, the British author.

"Sephra!" Johnny cried out. "You don't have to obey that ultimatum. You're going to stay here on this island!"

But Sephra just shook her head sadly. "I can't. My father has already packed everything and we are scheduled to leave tomorrow by emergency order of the government."

Nine

There was a lunar eclipse on the night of the move. The island sky was lit up with a sickly pink light as cart-full after cart-full of baggage was hurriedly carried away. Rumors of an outbreak of war spread throughout the island. Johnny took it into his head that he would take Sephra and the robin to a "another island" so they could all live together, even if he had to abduct her. He didn't know if he could live without her. Words the robin gave Sephra a message from Johnny. He wanted Sephra to remain in the Consulate until everyone had left and then hide there until he came for her.

The move resembled an evacuation on the eve of war. The Consul General's family loaded all their belongings onto their assigned wagons and set off for the headlands wharf. Resembling the Jack of Clubs, Sergeant Tomorrow, the all-too-serious man in charge of the move, shouted out loudly. "Everyone out as quickly as possible. As soon as everyone is out, we set fire to the estate!"

Ten

Johnny waved the flag decorated with black wings, which was the signal. This was the plan: when he waved the flag, Sephra was to slip out the back gate, get into the wagon which would be waiting there, and they would go in the opposite direction from the headlands wharf, to a bay where they would sail to another island. There were mountains of kindling stacked up around the estate.

"No one is left inside?" shouted Sergeant Tomorrow.

"Hey, Johnny," said Words. "We can't get Sephra out of there. Can't we just go alone, just the two of us?"

"Absolutely not," said Johnny shaking his head. "I don't want to live without Sephra."

"If everyone has exited the building, then we will begin the next stage of operations." Sergeant Tomorrow's voice gushed from the megaphone as he gave this last warning. With this announcement, the gatekeeper and the lazy old cat came tumbling out.

"Okay, that's everyone! No one else is inside!"

Just to be on the safe side, Johnny asked Words the robin to go see if Sephra had indeed slipped out the back gate or not. Words made one cursory flight around the grounds and came right back.

"Everything is okay," reported Words. "She is standing by herself outside the gate looking lonely and miserable."

Johnny didn't notice the robin's vaguely sad expression.

"I see," said Johnny. "Let's watch them set fire to our last memories of this Consulate and then be on our way."

Eleven

Finally, they set fire to the buildings. The flames spread before their eyes, lighting up the sky in brilliant crimson. Johnny drew Words close to his burnished cheek, and watched the fire, mesmerized. He did not begin to imagine, even in his wildest dreams, that his first love, Sephra, was being burned in the conflagration.

Sephra had waited for Johnny's flag signal, but she hadn't

CRIMSON THREAD OF ABANDON

been able to make out the black-winged flag in the black of the night. She had pleaded with Words, who had flown round, "Get Johnny to wave the flag as fast as you can! They'll put off setting fire to the place for a few more minutes . . ." But Words never mentioned any of this to Johnny.

Tomorrow morning, Johnny will probably weep in loud lamentation when he discovers the charred remains of his Sephra (his precipitate seventeen-year-old love). Thus this tale of a young man, a young woman and a robin will end.

This is a heartbreaking story of how learning to speak is synonymous to learning to lie. Johnny did not know that was precisely what Words the robin had learned.

MEMORY SHOTS

How many miles until I reach the memories?
I set out alone with a candle and my carriage.
Have I arrived or not?
How many miles until I reach the memories?
How many miles until the memories?

Yawn—I'm so bored. It has got to be my hundredth yawn today. I yawn so much that robins occasionally fly in and clean my teeth for me.

Since we opened our little clinic called "Memory General" in this port town, we have only had ten patients—in ten years! I have often chided the chief doctor for the ineffective sign: "Memory General."

Memories should rightfully be treated by eye, ear, nose and throat docs, I tell him; the reason being that memories are related to things like music and perfume. But the Chief will have none of it. Still, "Memory General" is just not right. I suggested that it makes more sense to call it Sight/Memory Center or Memory Psychiatry. But the Chief still maintains that "Memory General" is what he wants.

So, all the nurses quit, the pharmacist washed his hands of us. Even the cat, Alcohol, up and went somewhere, leaving just the Chief and me.

I told him, "Memory General" is grammatically wrong, so

he should switch it to "General Memory." But at the end of the day, he still stubbornly insists that "General" refers to the general practice and not memory in general.

Who am I? My name is Cotton Bawl, age sixty-one, second-in-command of this clinic, custodian, and security officer.

Mr. Who-am-I.

> What to do about an unpopular hospital?
> A fly laid six eggs in an untended syringe.
> I guess I have no choice but to
> go to London to buy some patients.

The entrance bell rang. Cotton Bawl thought it was someone playing tricks on him again. He paid no attention, but it rang again three more times in succession. The Chief and Cotton exchanged glances, and the doctor gave the signal to open the door. Cotton looked incredulous, but shrugged his shoulders and walked toward the door as slowly as possible. In short, he wanted to spare the visitor disappointment for as long as he could. He opened the door in slow motion. Standing there was a man in a tattered old raincoat.

"What can I do for you?" asked Cotton.

The man responded in a low, almost inaudible voice, "Is this the Memory General?" "This is the place," said Cotton.

"Can I get an examination at this hour?"

Cotton couldn't believe his ears, and he was about to welcome the man in gleefully, when he caught himself. He realized he should go through the motions of conferring with the Chief first, so he said, "Please wait here. I'll check."

When Cotton got to the back room, the doctor had already changed into his white coat and before Cotton could speak he said, "Show him in. I'll examine him."

The man in the worn-out raincoat came in looking for all the world like a ghost, and whispered, "I don't know anymore . . ."

"What is it you don't know?" asked the Chief.

"I don't know who I am anymore."

The Chief pulled out his stethoscope as if to do a real examination, but it was covered with dust and detritus and didn't appear functional.

"I have set out on this journey to find out who I am. But no one so far has been able to tell me. Then, when I happened to drop into this bar at the harbor called The Shoe Ship, the hostess there, named Gauze, told me about this clinic where she used to be a nurse. She told me that Memory General gives injections of memories. She said that instead of living with a nondescript history, you can make a happy life for yourself by having them inject your body with a pleasant past." The man in the raincoat was the soul of earnestness.

"Please, I beg you. I don't care whose memories they are. Inject me with genial ones."

Switched Memories—Crime in the Darkness

> What is in the bottle?
> Inside it is pitch black.
> Two stars twinkled.
> A kitten was crying
> because it can't get out.

The Chief gestured toward the bottles arranged all along the shelf saying, "Choose any one you want. They are all pleasant memories. Read the labels and make your choice."

The man in the raincoat was astonished by the huge variety of memories to be had. There were romantic memories labeled, "Galapagos Islands—A Balloon Journey for Two," "Premier Dance Performance—Dancing with Young Gacela," "One Hundred Kisses in a Day—Beloved Belladonna." The man in the raincoat carelessly took one from among them. It was labeled, "Meeting again in the Mediterranean—Madrigals in the Rain." This bottle contained the first half of the life of a young man who grew up at the Consulate in Acapulco who was reunited with the girl next door and they become engaged. The label read, "We are so happy now that we would like to share our past good fortune with others." It was even signed by the two sweethearts.

The man in the tattered old raincoat would be able to immerse himself in those memories, by appropriating the fictitious past in which he was supposed to have been born in the Consulate in Acapulco. He handed the bottle to Cotton saying, "Inject me with this one."

However, Cotton had a mean streak in him. Surreptitiously he switched the memory vile for a different one and innocently proceeded to fill the syringe. Maybe Cotton was vexed that someone else was headed for happiness. Perhaps he was just creating an incident simply because he was bored. No matter what his motivation was, the past he gave the man was a memory called "The Ventriloquist who Murdered Dummies."

Over Seven Pumpkins

> I fled from my shadow and
> leapt over seven pumpkins.
> Where, oh where
> is a town without memories?

26

"Thank you," said the man in the raincoat, and he left the clinic. He had no reason to believe that he had not been given the "Meeting again in the Mediterranean" memory injection. His mood had somehow cleared, the air was sweet and he felt like whistling. But . . . but . . . but.

No sooner had he come out on the street and taken a few steps when suddenly he had a strange feeling that someone was following him. He looked behind him to see who it might be. Something flitted through his mind. It might be the girl with the doll. The man suddenly remembered the French doll he murdered thirty years ago.

It was when he was still working the nightclub circuit as a ventriloquist. The man's dummy, Jinta, had fallen in love with that young girl's French doll and wouldn't listen to a thing the man said. Even in the middle of their act Jinta would blurt out, "I love Iris!" (the doll's name) or "I can't stand doing this act anymore!" which tended to rile the audience.

If a ventriloquist can't get on with his dummy, that finishes the act for all intents and purposes. He was eventually blackballed at all the clubs and had no way of making a living. The man was fed up. He wanted to teach Jinta a lesson, so he took a pair of scissors and cut up the French doll, Iris, leaving her in pieces.

From that time on, he wandered aimlessly, but he was constantly fearful of the French doll's shadowy presence around him. He always had the feeling that the girl to whom the French doll belonged, an adult now (although she retained her visage of adolescence), was following him. It was as if she were brandishing a pair of scissors, seeking revenge for the murder of her doll.

Did he hear footsteps behind him? Looking over his

shoulder he thought he was hallucinating: did he see snapping scissors emerging from behind a telephone pole. "I can't stand it anymore!" he cried and started to run. He was so frightened that it didn't occur to him that this "past" was what he had just been injected with. If I don't get out of here, she'll murder me, he thought. She'll cut me up into pieces just like I cut up Iris. He actually leapt over seven pumpkins and ran for his life toward a hotel on the outskirts of town.

To fiction with love

> How many miles until I reach the memories?
> I run barefoot
> Barked at by dogs and soaked in the rain.
> Have I arrived or not?
> How many miles until I reach the memories?

He got a room at the dilapidated old hotel called The Seagull. He lay down on the bed and had just breathed a sigh of relief when a knock came at the door. He caught his breath. Did she follow me all the way here? He shook with fear.

"Who's there?" he asked.

"It's me, dear," said an unfamiliar voice. "Open the door."

The voice sounded kind, so the man relaxed a little and opened the door part way. A beautiful woman he had never seen before stood before him holding a bouquet of flowers.

"It's me, dear," said the woman.

"I think you must be mistaken," said the man.

He had never seen this person before in his life. The woman, however, paid no attention to this and went about straightening up the room saying, "Your raincoat is so wrinkled", and "You've left socks all over the place." It was almost as if she were his wife, his real wife, of many years.

Perhaps this woman was injected with the posthumous memories of the "The Wife of the Raincoat Man," so she was entirely "the wife" in her heart, but not at all in appearance. They looked at each other and smiled, each living the life of different injections. Both were bewildered and lonely. They knew intuitively that they should make their peace together.

"Well, as long as you've come . . ." said the man in the raincoat warming up to her a little, "shall we have a glass of wine together?"

The woman nodded with the delight of a school girl.

"How lovely to grow old," she said.

"Why do you say that?" asked the man.

"Because you make just that many more memories."

GOTTA DANCE

My hand was writing on its own.
My feet were dancing on their own.
And I was left all alone.
Can't sleep at night.
Slight of hand.

Mizue intended to write the number 1. For some reason, however, her hand wrote the number 2. Then Mizue thought, "Ah ha. '1' is such a lonely number that my hand added one of its own accord. If you think of it as just a common mistake, then there is nothing to be worried about."

Mizue gently reproved her hand, erased the number 2 and once again attempted to write the number 1. Still, her hand ended up writing the number 2.

This wasn't the worst of it. From that day on Mizue's hand would not behave at all. For instance, Mizue did her best to practice the Bruno Mugellini Exercise #1 for Violin as her teacher had instructed, but her hands played "The Writhing Crocodile", which she had never played before in her life. Her teacher was quite taken aback and chastised her saying, "What a vulgar piece."

Mizue had a mind to explain that she certainly had not intended to play such a piece, but presuming that her teacher would not understand, she thought better of it. Instead she said, "Forgive me. I'll try again." She made a serious attempt to play the Mugellini exercise, but when she was finished she had played the tune called "The Pregnant Chimera." Finally, the teacher got angry.

"Bring your bottom over here. Your punishment is a beating with a bow!"

Footloose

No more than three days after her hands would no longer do her bidding, Mizue's feet began to thwart her. Saturday morning, she intended to visit Uncle Burrow in the hospital, but her feet walked her off to the aquarium where she found herself standing in front of the anchovy tank.

"Hi there," said Mizue. "Actually, I didn't really come here to see you, if the truth were known."

The anchovy families ground their teeth in consternation. "Well, nuts to you, too!" That was the end of that encounter. I mean really . . . just what kind of romance could take shape between a fifteen-year-old girl and a school of anchovies?

Mizue puzzled over why she ended up at the aquarium. Even assuming that her feet had eschewed a visit to the hospital, they must have had some pressing reason for bringing her to the anchovy tank at the aquarium. Nothing seemed probable no matter how much she thought about it. It occurred to Mizue to ask her feet, but she wasn't sure what language they spoke.

The next day, Mizue planned to go to the Rose Garden to see the roses there. But, as she feared, her feet walked away with her to Chinatown and up the stairs to the old fortune teller on the second floor over the pool hall. The old fortune teller pointed to the deck of cards on the dilapidated table before her and said, "Choose a card and turn it over."

Mizue attempted to turn over the second card from the top of the deck, but once again her hand would not obey her and turned over the seventh card from the bottom. It was a heart. "There is someone special to you in your life, am I right?" said the old woman. "But, if you don't confess your love soon, he will be whisked away by another girl."

How to Tell Him?

The young man Mizue loved was an assistant horse trainer. His job was to care for and ride thoroughbreds. He exercised the horses every morning to maintain their conditioning and weight.

In the morning fog at the track, just seeing this young man dismount from a brisk ride on a white horse, perspiration glistening on his forehead, made Mizue's heart pound. Occasionally, he too would look toward Mizue and grin, but they never spoke nor did they know each other's names.

Mizue resolved to write him a letter. She was convinced, however, that her hand would write something entirely different from what she intended. This made her afraid to write the letter at all. Mizue would have been content to keep things status quo, but the fortune teller's prediction stuck in her mind.

"If you don't confess your love for him, he will be whisked away by another girl," she had said, but who could this "other girl" be? Mizue became quite unsettled by even the thought of the other girl being prettier than she, and that the young man might fall in love with her instead. She knew she had to do something, but fifteen-year-old Mizue had no idea how to "confess her love."

That night, Mizue sat on her bed reading as usual. The book was *Justine* by the Marquis de Sade.[1] She had wanted to read *The Little Bookroom* by Eleanor Farjeon,[2] but her unruly hand selected de Sade's book.

Mizue was becoming accustomed to doing what her hands dictated. At dinner she really wanted to have some salad, but her hand chose cold cuts; and though she wanted grapefruit lemonade, her hand lifted a glass of wine to her lips. Her feet betrayed her as well.

In the middle of the night when everyone was sound asleep, Mizue was completely outdone with her feet, when they made her slip out of bed and dance about the house indiscriminately. She danced on all night, without the benefit of music. Mizue was exhausted. She tried to tie her feet to the bed, but now her hands would not cooperate. It seemed that her hands and feet were in cahoots.

"This is not the real me," whispered Mizue. "I'm trapped."

And it was true. Sadly enough, Mizue had become imprisoned in her own body.

> Who is trapped in
> the cabbage leaf?
> Who is trapped in
> the cargo ship of shoes?
> Who is trapped between
> page 23 and 24?
> Come find me,

---

1. 1791 novel set in the French Revolution about a young woman who defends herself against accusations of crime by explaining the ill-fortune she suffered which led to her current circumstances.

2. 1955 collection of children's stories featuring mythical and folk-loric characters such as kings, princesses, giants, a little dressmaker, and fairies.

oh, detective with the magnifying glass!
The real me, trapped in my body
weeps on.

I Want to Love, But Can't

"Do you think it was really your hands and feet that misbehaved?" asked Uncle Burrow. "Maybe your hands and feet were honest about what you wanted to do, and your head was being contrary." Mizue was brought up short. She had never thought about it that way.

"You have put your trust in your head, but your head isn't always to be believed." Perhaps he's right, she thought. Perhaps it had been hasty of her to assume that her "self" could be equated with her head. Mizue considered in her own mind . . . but then again wasn't her mind her head? . . . The more she thought the more confused she became.

The next morning when Mizue was walking along, deep in her own thoughts, the young man astride the white horse approached from the other direction. He was wearing shorts, and was barefoot.

"'Morning," he greeted Mizue.

"'Morning," she responded blushing at this unexpected meeting.

She thought this might be her only chance and was suddenly overwhelmed by a feeling of urgency.

"Uh . . ." Mizue faltered.

The young man looked down at her from atop the horse, grinning.

She meant to say, "I love you," but all that came out was, "I hate you." Mizue herself nearly cried out in dismay, and

34

the young man appeared to be stunned. Finally even Mizue's mouth had betrayed her.

The flustered Mizue tried again, and this time she succeeded. "I love you."

The young man became more and more bewildered. How does one respond to being told "I hate you" and then "I love you" in quick succession?

The young man, looking rattled, put his whip to his horse and dashed away at a good clip. Mizue was left standing there not knowing what to do.

There was no mistake about it: Mizue had said both, "I love you" and "I hate you." But which had the real Mizue said? "Just once in my life, I want to meet the real me," she thought.

> A woman's body is a castle.
> One little girl is hiding inside.
> "Ready or not, here I come!"
> But a castle is too vast for one's self,
> to play hide-and-seek.

Mizue will probably discover "herself" when she grows up, but for the time being she surrenders. She decided to let her hands, feet, and mouth determine her behavior. She did wish, however, that this trio would create just one more chance for her to say "I love you" to the young man. Here ends this disheartening story of first love.

THE ERASER

Soliloquy of Old Man Thumbs the Casket Maker

So, you noticed? Half of Smokey's tail (that's the cat) is missing. I inadvertently erased it, ha ha. I ran the eraser lightly over his tail and it just disappeared.

It wasn't just the cat's tail, though. I actually rubbed out my wife with a few quick strokes. So, here I am, now—a pathetic widower with no one to talk to but a cat. I know I'm the laughing stock of Nail-pull Alley, but this whole mess isn't my fault. It all started with that evil eraser.

> Old Man Thumbs the Casket Maker is a
> mean old drunk.
> He got wasted and rubbed out his wife.
> He rubbed her out with a few quick strokes.
> Only the harbor seagulls saw him do it.

Soliloquy of Johnny the Sailor

When I heard that story I thought, what a strange eraser. I mean, what is this weird thing, anyway? The erasers I used in school only erased pencil marks, but this one can rub out a living, breathing person or a cat's tail. So, I got Old Man Thumbs the Casket Maker to tell me where he got it. "I'll tell you where to find it, but don't go rubbing me out afterward," he said as I slipped him a large bottle of saké in exchange for information about the secret antique shop. It was called The Owl, the oldest (and almost bankrupt) shop in the harbor that dealt mainly in pirate booty. I set right out to find it.

> Johnny the Sailor wants an eraser.
> What does he want to rub out?
> What does he want to rub out?
> Only the harbor seagulls know for sure.

Soliloquy of The Owl Proprietor

Yes, yes, yes. This is the last eraser left. Use it wisely. And don't ask me where it was made, what it's made of, or who owned it before, because I don't know anything about it. As you can see, I am mostly deaf and nearly blind. Once I sell this eraser, I'm going to close up this shop and leave for some place far away. The Owl built its reputation on trust. I have sold everything imaginable in the last fifty years and, frankly, I'm tired of it.

Oh, I just remembered. I guess I should tell you how to use this eraser. Ready? Get a pane of glass and hold it up in front of the thing you want to erase. Sight it through the glass and rub it out as you would something on paper. Erase the object just like you would pencil marks. That's it. Hah, ha, ha...

Narrative by Me, the Author

Johnny the Sailor stuffed the eraser in his pocket and went home delighted. He strode on whistling, when he rounded a corner to find three swallows on the power lines overhead.

"Let's test the abilities of this eraser," said Johnny, and he proceeded to prop a pane of glass on the sign outside the liquor store. He crouched down so he could sight up to the swallows through the glass and then began to rub vigorously. Gradually the real birds faded and disappeared as if they had been no more than a faint pencil drawing.

> They disappeared.
> They disappeared.
> The swallows disappeared.
> The nefarious eraser takes the stage.
> Enter Madame Saturday

There was a reason why Johnny the Sailor wanted to get his hands on the "almighty" eraser. To shed light on this, I must first introduce Madame Saturday.

Madame Saturday—From the moment Johnny the Sailor laid eyes on her, he became slave to his lust for this woman, or should I say madam, cloaked in black garb emitting a mysterious charm resembling that of the old German movie actress Hildegard Knef. No one seemed to know her real name, where she lived, or anything about her. Yet, every Saturday she would appear in town whistling, hips swaying as she promenaded. Once she gave Johnny a wink as he passed her going the other way, which shot through him like electricity. She even disturbed his dreams that night.

In one dream, Madame Saturday was devouring bright red rose petals as she rode Johnny horse-style. Johnny was bridled (and probably naked) and was supposed to do Madame Saturday's bidding, but whatever surface he was on was unstable, making it impossible for him to make any forward progress. He remained on all fours, but every time he tried to move, an old sailor melody came wafting up from under him. Then he realized he was on a grand piano floating at sea. Frantically he tried to maintain his balance; one false move and he, the horse, and his rider, Madame Saturday, would sink into the ocean.

The Confession of Fan-Fan, Traveling Actor with the Eyeball Drama Troupe

You're in love? I don't think so, Johnny. First of all, she's too old for you. And you can't even begin to imagine that you could monopolize her affections. You don't have a penny to your name, and she looks like she has expensive tastes. Rumor has it that she has lots of other men like Captain One Eye, Ivan Gordonov the Taxidermist, and Tattoo-Jack the Diver.

Madame Saturday isn't a one-man kind of woman. An innocent like you couldn't possibly handle her. You can't buy her rings; you don't even have enough money to get her drunk. You can't make her go weak in the knees by crooning, either. You don't have a big, strong body to make love to her. Give up. It's for your own good.

> He fell in love with Madame Saturday.
> He sighed all Monday.
> He sighed all Tuesday.
> He sighed all Wednesday.
> He sighed all Thursday.
> He sighed all Friday.
> What to do, what to do?
> Only the harbor seagulls know.

Narration by Me, the Author

Johnny came up with an idea for possessing the beautiful Madame Saturday. He would use his eraser to rub out the all the other men she was seeing, one by one. Then, he thought, he would be the only one left, and she would be nice to him.

So, on a night when the moon hung in the sky like a recording of the old chanson "One Inebriated Evening," Johnny set out with his eraser and pane of glass. He wore a hunting cap pulled down low over his eyes and baggy pants, a disguise appropriate for the nefarious eraser. His first target was Captain One Eye.

There he was, sitting on a rum barrel, a red dog at his side, with a thumb-shaped pipe in his mouth, waiting for Madame Saturday. Johnny apologized to Captain One Eye in his heart, and then set about rubbing him out fast and furious. Fast and furious. Gradually, the figure of Captain One Eye faded and finally disappeared altogether.

Madame Saturday arrived late, and was astonished to find nothing but a pair of rubber boots Johnny had neglected to erase. Captain One Eye was nowhere to be seen. She looked around and saw Johnny standing there, grinning.

Johnny used the same method to rub out Ivan Gordonov the Taxidermist and his Hideaway Hearse. When Madame Saturday arrived and looked around, there was Johnny grinning.

Johnny used the same method to rub out Tattoo-Jack the Diver and the White Horse, Endurance. When Madame Saturday arrived and looked around, there was Johnny grinning.

Finally, Madame Saturday deigned to speak to Johnny. "Come to the South Pacific Hotel tomorrow."

A Man Through the Keyhole?

Johnny headed out with his arms full of red roses. His heart danced at the prospect of his clandestine meeting with Madame Saturday. But when he got to the door of her room, he heard a man's voice inside. He couldn't believe his ears for a moment, but there was no mistake. Johnny peeked through the keyhole just in time to see the back of someone getting into the bathtub.

Johnny was filled with jealous rage. He'd had it all nicely worked out so he could be alone with Madame Saturday, and now someone had beaten him to it. He took out the eraser and the pane of glass, put it up against the keyhole and began rubbing passionately.

"That'll fix you! You're finished!

When he was done, he opened the door and went in. But, alas, no one was there. There was only a radio on the bed tuned to a male baritone voice. Johnny realized, then, that the voice he had heard had been on the radio. So the figure he had erased had been—yes, there was no doubt—none other than Madame Saturday.

> A blunder.
> A blunder.
> A blunder.
> I rubbed out Madame Saturday.
> What shall I do?
> What shall I do?
> Tell me what to do
> Harbor seagulls of the blue moon!

Johnny wept, realizing that he had made an irreparable mistake. He felt he had no recourse but to follow Madame Saturday into oblivion and rub himself out as well. He stood in front of the mirror and began to erase himself. He had used up a good portion of the eraser already, though, so he had only erased half his body when the eraser ran out entirely.

So with a blue moon in the harbor sky, this sorrowful Johnny the Young Sailor, only half the man he had been, rubbed out from the waist down, set out on a journey to find a new eraser, weeping all the way.

The Elusive Milena

The Photographer Resembled Frankenstein

It was an average, everyday photography shop, but there was just one thing odd about it. It wasn't that the owner vaguely resembled Frankenstein, or that real stardust flew up when he used his magnesium flash. There was just something odd about the photos he produced.

> The moon appeared
> In a photo
> Taken on a
> moonless night.
> Who put it there?

"I don't believe it," exclaimed the Chinese barometer maker, as he looked at the photograph.

"I don't look that old! And I don't have a beard either. What's going on?"

Upon inspection, the man in the photo had white hair and was slightly bent, though the Chinese barometer maker in real life was quite young.

The barometer maker was holding the photograph, his hands shaking violently, when the owner of the photography shop (who actually does vaguely resemble Frankenstein) whispered devilishly into his ear, "My camera takes pictures that show what things will look like ten years in the future."

"What!" said the barometer maker, incredulous. "Is this supposed to be me, ten years down the road?"

"Yes," answered the shop owner. "Congratulations. You will apparently still be alive in ten years . . ."

"But, but . . ." The barometer maker peevishly ran his hands through his hair. "Damn, it looks like I didn't get rich!"

> In a blue back street photo, created
> by the magnesium ghoul,
> The shutter clicks and one disappears.
> The shutter clicks and two disappear,
> The shutter clicks and three disappear.
> Then everyone is out of the picture.
> A picture of nothing!

A Baby at the International Hinge Expo?

Rumors about this photography shop did not spread as one might have expected. It wasn't well patronized. There was one poster of a commonplace sailor up in the window (something like a bromide of George Raft[1] in the western sunset) covered with dust because the proprietor never bothered to clean the place.

Nonetheless, occasionally a young couple would come in asking him to take a picture of them "ten years in the future."

One day a poor craftsman, who had won a prize for his submission of storybook hinges at the International Hinge Expo, and his girlfriend, who was an artist, came to the shop. Both were extremely nervous.

"They say the photo will show us ten years from now . . ." the craftsman ventured to say. "Maybe I'll end up a poor hobo."

---

1. George Raft (1901–1980) was an American film actor known for his gangster roles.

"I guess I could end up as a poor prostitute trying to get tricks at some godforsaken dive," she said a little embarrassed.

The two stood together fidgeting bashfully, when suddenly the magnesium flash flared and a white dove appeared.

"Oh my, a baby!" the hinge craftsman said spontaneously.

The photograph showed the craftsman and his sweetheart (much more well-dressed), and between them a little boy wearing a sailor suit. The lovers clasped their hands together. The sweetheart whispered shyly, "I wish we could smile to the end of the world."

The Gambling Gentleman's Dice for Death

"The shutter is what makes the camera blink," said the photography shop owner. "It is a moment of eternity. In ancient India, blinking was a way of explaining the incredible speed of the cosmos. They said that the universe can leap 2,057,152 *yojana*[2] in the form of a common harbor seal in the time it takes God to blink."

"If the existence of the universe is explained in terms of God blinking, then it seems that my future will be determined by the Devil blinking," replied the Gambling Gentleman, who was dressed in a frock coat. He was tall, dark, and shadow-like (and had been playing the lottery since the day he was born). This man had his picture taken twice, but the photo came out blank both times.

"Now stop that," said the photography shop owner. "Even if you don't exist ten years from now, you would think that at least a stone cross or a handful of dirt might show up."

"Actually, if I cease to exist, then I'd rather have everything disappear as well," said the Gambler.

2. Measure of distance used in ancient India. One *yojana* is equivalent to approximately eight miles.

"But, what I really want to know is if I will die ten years from now or five years from now," he said as he took a die out of his frock coat pocket and rolled it on the table. A "4"[3] came up (and perhaps that meant "for death").

"Ah, death," said the shop owner.

To which the Gambler replied, "Yes, but look. This die has only fours." He held out the die to the shop owner. Each side of the die had only four black dots. The Gambler walked out of the photography shop and had not gone more than ten meters down the road when, unfortunately, he was hit by the flower shop truck and died.

Finally the Protagonist, the Flutist Young Bunn Appears

> In the cellar of the photo shop
> There were seven bottles
> Filled with darkness
>
> Poke seven holes
> With a colored pencil
> And there you have seven stars

Jun, a member of the explorers club, said, "What if you could adjust the length of your projected future any way you wanted in the same way you focus the lens of a camera?"

"Then you could know everything about yourself from tomorrow to a hundred years in the future."

"If you could do that . . ." said the man with black-rimmed glasses, "I'd buy this photography shop on the spot."

Well, how about that? That very man with the black-rimmed glasses was a spy from a life insurance company.

---

3. Though the characters are different, "4" (四) is a homophone for "death" (死), both pronounced "shi" (し).

I know this is breaking the rules, but I think it is about time for the protagonist of this story to make his entrance. This would be the rather unsuccessful flutist known as Young Bunn. Every day Bunn would go to the railway station and make pocket change by playing his bamboo flute for people who were bidding each other farewell. He wore a cardboard sign around his neck which read:

> I will play a farewell song for you.
> A happy farewell—6 guilders
> A short farewell—5 guilders
> A pitiful farewell—4 guilders
> A sad farewell—3 guilders
> A bittersweet farewell—2 guilders
> A painful farewell—1 guilder
>
> No farewells—Free
> (The length of the song will be determined by the length of the farewell)

Travelers who were leaving on long journeys were delighted with his music. Bunn himself, however, had never bid farewell to anyone in his life. He thought that he would very much like to play his gull flute for himself just once.

But before you can say good-bye you must meet someone first. He had neither friend nor sweetheart. He kept telling himself, "I may be a roving flute-player now, but I am going to be a great composer in the future."

One day, on a whim, Bunn went into the photography shop. He decided to have the owner (vaguely resembling Frankenstein) take just one photo of him.

I don't know if he intended to send it home to his relatives or if he was just going to put it in his wallet. In any case, he washed his tired old sweater, washed his face three times, and went to the photography shop. Click! The shutter snapped.

"Who is this?!" he exclaimed, when he saw the picture. There was a lovely looking girl standing next to him whom he did not recall ever having seen. Quite taken aback, he looked about him, but there was no one there.

"There is a person in the picture who wasn't there when you took it," he said. The owner replied, " Oh, that's Milena."

"Who is this Milena?" asked Bunn.

"The person you are going to meet," said the owner. "I don't know anything about her." Bunn was delighted with the photo which predicted that he would be with this girl Milena in ten years. It wasn't too late for him. He took the photo in hand and dashed out into the town.

> Oh Robin, Oh Robin!
> Do you know where
> My eraser went?
> Do you know where the
> Lost memories of my Milena went?
>
> I know I'll find her someday;
> Maybe tomorrow, the next day
> Or year after next.
> Have you seen the girl, Milena,
> Who is knitting a bright
> White sweater?

Gentle reader, Milena is a pseudonym. If a young flute-player comes up to you and calls you "Milena," please speak to him. It will most likely be the moment captured in that photo taken ten years ago.

REMY'S QUANTUM REALITIES

Smokey the Cat Is Hungry

It all started with the blind, old accordion player on one of the back streets. Remy had gone out to buy milk for Smokey the cat, when she was hailed by the old accordion player. "Listen to just one song before you go," he said. "I won't take much of your time. It's a beautiful love song. I just composed it—it's brand new."

"I can't really—" said Remy. "I've come out this late at night because my cat, Smokey, is hungry and he's waiting for me to bring this milk home."

She was about to move on, when the old accordion player began to cry.

"No one will listen to my songs. I've been waiting here three days and everyone just passes me by. I guess no one wants to listen to any song of mine . . ." Remy felt sorry for him. Yet, she couldn't ignore Smokey who was waiting for her. She wanted to hear the old man's song, but she also wanted to get the milk to her cat. Ultimately, she decided in favor of Smokey because he was sick. So, though she didn't want to disappoint the old man, she took her precious bottle of milk and began to hurry home.

After walking a little way, Remy thought she heard the old man singing somewhere behind her. Who else could have passed by him this late at night, she wondered to herself; but when she looked around she was astonished by what she saw.

Who should be sitting down with a bottle of milk in her arms listening to the old man's love song, but Remy herself.

"I don't believe it!" she blurted out. But it was neither an illusion nor a case of mistaken identity. When the blind old man sang,

> The child jumped over the spoon
> The red weather vane twirled

it was none other than Remy who joined him in the refrain, "twirled and twirled." "Wait a minute," she thought. "If that is Remy over there, then who am I?"

Before It's Too Late

The strange events did not end there. Remy returned to her apartment, deep in thought, and opened the door to find all the lights out.

"Smokey?" she called out softly. "I brought you your milk."

Then, though no one should have been there, a sleepy voice came from Remy's bed, "Who's there?"

The shocked Remy lifted the lamp off the table (a lamp she had just purchased from the Sundries Antique Shop) "More to the point, who are you?" she retorted.

"I'm Remy," said the girl on the bed. Remy approached, the lamp in hand, and there was another Remy sitting on the bed (it was almost like looking in the mirror, unbelievable as it might sound).

"No, I'm Remy," said the Remy who had just come home.

"You have no business coming into my apartment without so much as a by-your-leave."

The Remy sitting on the bed was undeterred and shot back, "How dare you come waltzing into my apartment pretending to be me!" She lifted up the pumpkin alarm clock and said, "What time do you think it is? I'm going to call the police!"

"Call them!" said the Remy who had just come home. "Tomorrow I'll get all the neighbors to identify me! I'll get Subby the Sailor from next door, Madam Drinkwater the fortune teller from across the way, and the twin piano tuners two doors down, Aris and Totle (together they make ArisTotle). You'll see."

The Remy sitting on the bed remained undaunted, "Oh yeah? Well, the landlady, Mrs. Sixpence, the sewer worker Mr. Tarzan, and Spud Pythagoras at the dry goods store on the corner will all tell you I'm me!"

"They sure will," said the Remy who had just came home.

"The best way to tell who is who is to ask Smokey. He'll know his owner." The Remy sitting on the bed called out, "Smokey!"

"Which one of us is Remy?"

The sleepy cat raised his head and looked at the Remy on the bed. This Remy swelled with pride and confidently nodded her head.

Then Smokey looked at the Remy who had just come home. That Remy held out the bottle of milk and nodded with kindness. The cat suddenly shook its head sharply.

His ears and tail stood on end as if he couldn't believe his eyes as he quickly compared the two. He shut his eyes tight and opened them to compare the two again. He shook his head, trembled violently and jumped up. He leapt over the violin and out the window.

> The cat jumped over the violin
> But the moon pretended not to see
> Eat your fill of stew
> Before it's too late.

It's the Potato's Fault

The next morning the two Remys woke at almost the same moment. Both yawned, got out of bed, plugged in the coffee maker and then got a potato from a basket in the corner of the kitchen.

"Okay . . . ," began Remy. "Shall I make hash browns or boiled potatoes today?"

The other Remy said, "No, today I'm going to make either buttered skillet potatoes or mashed potatoes." In no time a contentious discussion ensued. "Traditionally, potatoes are best when fried or boiled," Remy insisted.

But the other Remy said, "The modern way of preparing potatoes is either to toss them in a skillet or steam and mash them." Neither Remy was going to back down.

Remy couldn't decide whether she wanted hash browns or boiled potatoes, and the other Remy couldn't decide if she wanted skillet potatoes or mashed potatoes. Then, Remy split into four people, and the potato was left languishing on the tabletop.

Boiled-Potato Remy said, "I'll fill this pot with water." Hash Brown-Remy said, "Tasting the grease with my pinky is such a bad habit." Mashed-Potato Remy said, "You've got to have music when you're cooking; something energizing with pizzicato in it." Skillet potatoes-Remy said, "Oh, I forgot! Today is Saturday!"

Finally, the four Remys and the one cat, Smokey, sat around the table eating their preferred potato dishes. This quartet didn't engage in conversation, however; rather they preferred to ignore the other three as best they could.

When breakfast was over, all four Remys clasped their hands behind their backs and paced around the room deep in thought. DeeDee, the French doll under the bed, was chewed up by mice, a result of living fast and loose. Smokey basked in the sun, and occasionally the local priest ran by the window as if running the hundred-yard dash.

Of the four Remys, one put a spoon in her pocket and mused about going for a walk, one put a spoon in her mouth and made faces in the mirror, one sang "Drop a spoon and a fool will come to your door," and one put a spoon under her pillow and chanted an incantation.

The doorbell rang twice. In came the mail carrier saying, "Special Delivery for Miss Remy." All four Remys bounded forward and together grabbed at the blue special delivery envelope. Finally, the Remy who got possession of the envelope looked at the sender's name. "Well," she said tossing it down, "It's not from anyone I know." At that moment, Remy came out of the kitchen saying, "Oh, it's a letter from my old friend Kamé."

"Oh my. That is a blast from the past. I'd nearly forgotten all about him."

The Remys who had forgotten him passed the letter slowly to the Remy who remembered him, and she opened it up.

Why the Burro Got Stuck in the Piano

"All right everyone, pay attention. (1) Two items that are the same are equal. (2) Add the same amount to any two equal items and they remain in equal harmony. (3) Subtract the same amount from any two equal items and the difference between them remains equal. (4) Two things mutually concordant are mutually equal. (5) The whole is larger than the constituent parts. These are Euclid's five axioms."[1]

Professor Zero, a man with a large pelican-like mouth, is teaching math class. The students attending class are each sitting at a desk, with the exception of the eight Remys, who are crowded onto one seat in a back-to-back scrum. (The number of Remys doubled when they had to decide to walk on the right side of the street or the left side of the street.) One Remy is bored in class and is daydreaming about a piano floating in a lake, while another Remy imagines herself cast in a French movie in which she is a captive in a castle dungeon.

Suddenly, one Remy dashed out into the schoolyard chasing an Agrias Butterfly, and another Remy remained in the classroom, so the teacher had no grounds for reprimand. At that same moment, there was a twelve-year old Remy who was fixing the red garter of her hooker-like outfit in the bathroom of the Chinese knife sharpener; and there was even a Remy who stowed away on a cargo ship to travel the world.

In the Botanical Gardens alone there were thirty-three Remys standing in front of thirty-three different varieties of flowers, and a Remy in her moonlit bedroom unsuccessfully practicing the violin and being punished by her teacher.

The number of Remys increased alarmingly, and has

1. A parody of Euclid's five postulates which appear in his first book, *Elements*.

probably increased two or three fold during the time it has taken me to write this story. This doesn't mean, however, that every girl in the world is named Remy. Here is your homework assignment. How many Remys appeared in this story? Write your answer on a piece of paper, put it in a small bottle and send it to me. When I get your answer, I'll tell you why the burro got stuck in the piano.

One-Centimeter Journey

One

The girl's name was Aris. The boy's name was Totle. Together they made Aris-n-Totle, or so everyone said.

Eventually, the "-n-" was elided and they were known as Aris-Totle. They were considered sweethearts by society at large, but Aris knew their love was not going to last forever. She knew this because of what Aristotle had said. "Perfection is replete; it is finite rather than complete."[2]

Two

Aris worked at a bookstore. She loved to switch books around on the shelves (on the sly so the shop owner wouldn't notice) depending on what was written on the spine. For instance, if *Homeless Child* were shelved next to *Frankenstein*, she would pull it off the shelf and place it next to *Old Man Long-legs*. She would put *The Man Who Lost His Shadow* next to *The History of Lighting*, and she took pleasure in the irony of putting *The Laughing Cat* between two copies of *Poems of a Certain Love*. Aris preferred old books to new ones, and was particularly partial to leather-bound classical poetry collections hand-written on parchment. (These she tried to avoid selling by

---

2. The notion of perfection as defined by Aristotle in the book *Delta* of *Metaphysics*.

hiding them unobtrusively on the top shelves of a remote corner.)

Three

Totle crafted mirrors. His job was to polish all the various type of mirrors made at the back street shop, Blinkers Mirrors, which handled everything from hand mirrors to huge wall mirrors, each priced accordingly. Among those the shop carried was one which only reflected the mirror holder even though they might be standing in a crowd of people; one which reflected couples as dogs, and one which would show only the holder's death mask. Totle kept all of the mirrors shiny and spotless. If one sold, he was responsible for delivering it to the customer's home. On occasion, he was asked to change the frame to accommodate the buyer's preference, or trim down a mirror which was too large. The most popular mirror was called the "Snow White", which made anyone appear to be the most beautiful person in the world. (Totle secretly wanted to buy one of these as a present for Aris when he had enough money saved up.)

> Aris, Totle and the moon
> All together make a tale.
> Take away one, you still have a tale.
> Take away two, you still have a tale.
> Take them all away, you still have a tale.
> May I offer you a pen?

Four

Aris was waiting, as was their routine, at the park for Totle, who arrived late. "What's this?" thought Aris. She wasn't wearing high heels, but Totle seemed slightly shorter than usual. "This is odd," thought Aris. "Did I get taller?" Usually, the top of Aris' head came up to Totle's cheek; nonetheless they now stood at the same height cheek to cheek.

"Is this the moon's trickery?" wondered Aris. "Or could this be a manifestation of Aristotle's notion of nature giving and taking away?" Aris went straight to *The Complete Encyclopedia of Size*, and looked up information about growth and shrinkage in human beings. Then she went to the Measure-All Company and had herself measured. She discovered that her height had not changed, so she concluded that Totle must have shrunk.

> Totle is a lazy boy
> One shoe on
> One pant leg on
> He has dropped his straw hat
> And while he was fast asleep
> Everyone in the world got taller.

Five

As unbelievable as it may sound, it was true that Totle had gotten a little shorter. This became clear on the second day, and on the third day there was no question about it, he was shrinking with no end in sight. Standing before the mirror that reflected the holder in their original form, Totle was at his wits end. "Am I shrinking or is everything else in the world expanding?"

Six

It was sad that Aris and Totle could no longer enjoy their time together as they had before. It was almost as if Aris was walking hand in hand with a chimpanzee when she was out with Totle who had shrunk to about her knees. The Three-penny tramp, passing by, pointed and laughed behind their backs as the two of them went into the Dark Moon dance hall. "A street performer and her chimp just went dancing!"

> Call a doctor when
> the broad bean falls ill.
> If the broad bean wants to die,
> pop the shell.
> Do you have any idea
> what I'm talking about?

Seven

Eventually, Totle was reduced to forty centimeters. All the mirrors felt sorry for him and had already stopped reflecting him, so he was unable to see how small he had become. He received an invitation to join the little people's "Forty Centimeters Club," but he turned them down. He also quit the job he had held for such a long time at Blinkers Mirrors. He would not see Aris, and shut himself up in his room.

He would not speak to anyone, but he had not stopped loving Aris; on the contrary, his love for her deepened. Yet, the large discrepancy in their heights made it quite daunting for him to be with her.

"Why won't you see me?" asked Aris over the phone.

"I don't want to see you," answered Totle.

"Don't you love me anymore?" asked Aris.

". . ."

"Come on, say something,"

"I've shrunk some more. I can't be any more than ten centimeters tall at this point."

"You must be adorable."

". . ."

"So, why won't you see me?"

"I couldn't stand your pity."

"Wh . . .What did you just say?"

"Just holding the receiver while we're talking is hard for me. It's heavy and a lot bigger than I am. I'm tiny and skinny; a lot like a half-used colored pencil. We won't be able to love each other even if we do get together. I could very well be sucked right into your mouth if we tried to kiss. I'm even terrified of flies now. It is like being targeted by a helicopter when they come buzzing around me.

"On windy days, I'm blown around, and who knows where I might get thrown by the force of a sneeze. Just the other day I was reading *The Chronicles of Narnia*[1] when the wind came up and I got sandwiched between the pages and couldn't get out. I'm sorry, but I want you to forget about me. If things continue on as they have been, it is only a matter of time before I shrink below one centimeter and get snuffed out all together."

Eight

> A tiny, tiny flower blossomed at the end of a
> tiny, tiny pencil.
> A tiny, tiny huge happening occurred!

One day, Aris discovered an odd but unobtrusive advertisement in the newspaper. It read like this.

"I will grant you one wish. This is only valid for two people who truly love each other. A wish will be granted to the first three who respond. Forefinger Friend."

---

1. A series of fantasy novels by C.S. Lewis.

Aris thought this was nonsense at first, but she was grasping at straws, and decided to visit this Forefinger Friend. Even if she had to hand over all of her worldly belongings, it would be worth it if she and Totle could be happily together again.

People who truly love each other are fairly rare, I'd say, thought Aris. She ventured out, the address in the newspaper advertisement in hand, to find the Forefinger Friend in a back street gypsy inn.

"I want to have a certain person made larger," said Aris, but the Forefinger Friend shook her head. "The wish must be a wish for yourself only."

So Aris told her she wanted to be made one centimeter tall. "Our anniversary, the day Totle and I first met is coming up soon. We promised we would go to the seventh bench in the park on that day. Please, I beg you. Make me shrink to one centimeter on that day."

Forefinger Friend acknowledged this, but set three conditions.

(1) You may never love another after this (in other words, you will receive all the love of the other person and use it freely). (2) Once the wish has been granted it cannot be reversed (no regrets). (3) The wish will not be granted if your love is not true, and you cannot hold this against the Forefinger Friend.

In addition, you must hand over all your belongings (anything valuable like rings, shoes, hats). This made Aris quite anxious, but she decided to risk it.

"I'll give you everything I own. Just grant my wish."

Nine

> Aris, Totle and the moon
> all together make a tale.
> Take away one, you still have a tale.
> Take away two, you still have a tale.
> Take them all away, you still have a tale.
> May I offer you a pen?

The appointed day when the two had promised to meet arrived. That morning when Aris woke up, she felt as if she were lying under a heavy board, but it was actually her blanket on top of her body, which had shrunk to one centimeter.

"Finally, my wish has come true, " cried Aris. Now they could become the one centimeter lovers. They would be happy just as they had been. Aris got herself all made up and left for the park which held so many memories for her. She could feel a warmth spread through her chest as she thought how happily surprised Totle would be and what he would say.

There came Totle, out from under the mottled sunlight coming through the sycamore trees. There he was, restored to his original size, carrying a bouquet of flowers for Aris in his hand. Aris looked up at him agog, but Totle didn't seem to see her.

"She is going to be so surprised," said Totle to himself. "When she sees that my wish came true and I am back to my normal size, I'll bet she'll cover me with a hundred kisses. Finally, today I'll be able to propose to her for real."

He looked at his watch, puzzled. "She's awfully late . . ."

Trying to avoid being stepped on, Aris stood weeping. She couldn't bring herself to call out to him, "It's me, Totle! Down here!"

What a mess. Aris hadn't foreseen that Totle might also go to Forefinger Friend to have his wish granted. "I guess I was right. We weren't meant for each other," she murmured.

Looking up at Totle, Aris went round and round his shoes like shimmering heat until she felt she was becoming so small she was about to disappear all together.

FIVE STORIES OF HIDE-AND-SEEK

Hiding Until Adulthood

"Let's play hide-and-seek!" It was the boy with green hair. No one knew his name or where he came from, but all the children gathered around anyway. They had been at loose ends and were just waiting for an invitation to play.

"Who's going to be 'it'?" Rock, paper, scissors—It was the boy with green hair who lost. "I always lose," said the boy, and stuck out his tongue. Then he covered his eyes and hunkered down to count. The children scattered to go hide.

"Are you ready?" said the boy.

"Not ready!" came a voice. The boy counted again from one to a hundred. "Are you ready?" he called, but this time there was no answer.

"Okay, I guess they're all set." The boy stood up and strode off without ever making a move to find the children hiding in the town.

That evening, there was a great uproar. The phone was ringing off the hook at the police station. One mother reported tearfully, "My child didn't come home tonight." There was a stunned middle school child who called in to say, "My little brother has disappeared." Several of the children who had played hide-and-seek remained hidden and never reappeared. A posse searched the entire town, but there was no trace of those children anywhere.

The next day, in another town at about the same time of day, a boy called out to the neighborhood children, "Let's play hide-and-seek!" It was the same boy with green hair. No one knew his name or where he came from, but all the children gathered around. "Who's going to be 'it'?" Rock, paper, scissors—It was the boy with green hair who lost. "I always lose," said the boy, and he became the seeker. He covered his eyes and hunkered down to count. "Are you ready?" he called out.

That evening, the children who hid were nowhere to be found. No one could figure out if the children had just vanished, or if they intended to stay hidden (for years to come) so they would never be found. In the days that followed, there were games of hide-and-seek in other towns and children vanished. Ultimately, every single last child in this country disappeared all together. Who was that green-haired boy?

In the sunlight of the evanescent autumn, I just happened to remember a passage from the picture book entitled *History*, written by a classical Spanish poet.

> Count a thousand nights,
> and the dead and hidden children
> will come back home as adults.

Confessions of an Old Seeker

"I've been a seeker for more than seventy years now," boasted the old man almost as if he expected to be recognized with an award for his many long years of service. Even on his business card, which he proffered, his title read, "Seeker for the Game of Hide-and-Seek."

When I asked, "Why have you been a seeker for such a long time?" he looked back sourly. "I make a point of not going to seek them.

"In the game of hide-and-seek, everyone has to stay hidden until the seeker spies them and shouts, "I found you!" They all want to come out as fast as they can, so they're waiting for me to show up.

"I know that they're hiding in the barn in a haystack, but I intentionally pretend not to know they're in there and pass them by. So they've been left there for seventy years still hiding in the haystack." The old man sniggered.

"But . . ." I continued, "don't you think seventy years is just too long? Why don't you go find them quickly?"

At this, the old man betrayed a remote sense of melancholy. "While they are hiding, they are still thinking about me. Not only that, they're waiting for me. Their lives are devoted to waiting just for me. But, if I find them, they'll forget about me in a heartbeat. Then I'll be all alone again." As if to cover his emotions, he laughed once more. It was a sharp laugh rather like squeaky shoes.

"Those guys who were hiding are still children. But look at me, I've become this old man. Seventy years seem to have passed in the twinkling of an eye."

For a brief moment, I thought I heard the children in the haystack far away in the old man's hometown call out, "We're ready! . . . We're ready!"

The old man had said it had been seventy years, but perhaps that was just his emotional perspective on the amount of time that had passed. It could be the few minutes from the time the sky turns crimson at twilight to sunset—children hide, dinner preparations are beginning at home, the horn of the tofu vendor resounds through the neighborhood as usual. The only one abandoned on the street is the little boy who plays the seeker.

Hide-and-seek is a lonesome game. The hiders and the seeker pass separate autumns, and they are greeted by separate winters. It is only memories which remain obscurely confined without the possibility of release. They call back and forth to each other, "Are you ready?" "Not yet!" "Are you ready?" "Okay, ready!"

Hide-and-Seek: The Double Suicide Only Seagulls Witnessed

It was a winter day. A man and a woman made their way to a remote promontory on the coast. The man had a violin case under his arm, and the woman had only her handbag. The woman laid her head on the man's shoulder, and the two gazed at the winter sea silently for a long time. Then, they faced each other and nodded. In the violin case he held at his side was not a violin, but rather there appeared to be something resembling a letter. The man opened the case, checked the contents and set it down on the rocks. He then took her hand. Fully clothed, they held each other and hurled themselves into the sea. The turbulent sea met the two and swallowed them in an instant.

After a time, the bittersweet voices of the two arose from the bottom of the ocean, "We're ready!"

"We're ready!"

"We're ready!"

Of course, no seeker would go to the ends of the earth to find such a couple. They were doomed never again to emerge from their fate.

The Endless Game: "Ready?!" "Not Yet!"

These two had been playing hide-and-seek for many years now. The young man always hid and the old man was always the seeker. On one occasion, the young man stole a harmonica from an antique shop. It was the old man who came after him. The young man dashed into an alley and hid in a vacant house. The old man approached and called out, "Ready?"

Several years after that, the young man fell in love with a married woman. The two boarded a train and fled to the young man's hometown. The woman was the wife of the old man. The cuckolded seeker followed them. The lovers hid in a whitewashed storehouse and did not emerge for days. The old man circled the storehouse time and time again calling out, "Ready?" Finally, the young man blurted out, "Not yet!" In that instant, the woman burst into tears. That was the final demise of their love affair.

A number of years passed when a series of unforeseen events led the young man to stab someone and run away. The police officer who pursued him was the old man.

On his way home, the old man chuckled and whispered, "I wonder how long this hide-and-seek game is going to go on?" As their encounters continued over the years, the young man gradually aged, and he began to feel an intense desire to actually see the old man. He did not have the slightest idea how to manage a meeting. He had no address, nor did he know the old man's profession. Suddenly it occurred to him to just shout out, "I'm ready!"

> "I'm ready!"
> "I'm ready!"
> "I'm ready!"

But, sadly the old man did not appear. What was this relationship between these two men? A certain moralist said it was a case of filial piety. A poet said the two were homosexuals. A mathematician said their relationship was a case of mere coincidence, and a spiritualist said their encounter was a matter of destiny. All this said, however, hide-and-seek is still hide-and-seek.

Thinking back over it all, hide-and-seek is a game in which the players take turns hiding and being the seeker. If it were left up to me, I would have the young man try calling out, "Ready?" for a change. We all forget sometimes that it is our turn to be the seeker.

There Is Always a Little Girl Hiding in the Mirror

If you want to play hide-and-seek by yourself, just look in a mirror. You cover your eyes while your mirror image hides. When you take your hands away and say, "Ready?" you will very possibly hear another voice say, "I'm ready."

The excitement of hide-and-seek is the notion of confinement. At some point, you stop seeking and leave the mirror. But, you keep repeating to yourself, "Not yet, not yet!" so that you can remain that little girl who lives in the mirror.

As always, it is only the seeker who ages.

ALICE IN SHADOWLAND

The Shadow Shop

"Okay, stand right there," said the man at the Shadow Shop. Alice did as she was told and stood on the large sheet of paper on the floor. By the light of the moon, Alice's shadow stood out sharply on the paper.

"Hold still just like that," said the man as he began powerfully to cut out Alice's shadow with large scissors that looked like tailor shears. It felt a little ticklish to Alice, much as it did the first time she went to the barber at No. 99. She didn't want any important part of her shadow to be sliced off, so she stood stock-still. Then the man shouted out, "Done!" He took the paper cutout of her shadow, rolled it up, and put it in a paper bag for her. "I feel lighter somehow," said Alice, "Thank you."

With her shadow in the bag, Alice danced her way home through the moonlit town. Yet no one looked at her and commented, "Poor child, she has no shadow," or "Did you leave your shadow somewhere?"

When Alice got home, she opened the door quietly and slipped inside. She expected her cat, Smokey, to be hungrily waiting for her to come home. The room was dark with only the light of the gas street lamp shining through a slight gap in the curtains. "Smokey, honey . . ." she called out. She took a step forward and just barely missed tripping over the speaker trumpet of the phonograph. "Where are you?" she said looking around the room. It was then that she noticed it. There was Alice's long, slim shadow reflected there on the floor.

"What the . . . ?" Alice blurted out. Although she had just had her shadow removed, another shadow was attached to her. Alice thought perhaps it was an oversight on her part, so she peered inside the paper bag. Sure enough, her shadow was still in the bag as it should have been. Alice turned the paper bag upside down and dumped out the shadow (much as one would dump out a newly purchased pair of trousers). The shadow was drawn to Alice magnetically and neatly attached itself to her feet. Alice was on the verge of tears. "Oh God! Now I have two shadows!"

The Cardboard Moon

"The two are exactly the same size. It is impossible to tell which is which," said the surveryor as he wound up his tape measure.

"You must have thought I was lying when I told you I had two shadows," replied Alice rather embarrassed. "What should I do?"

The surveyor suggested that she should go to the "Master Shadow Catcher." According to the surveyor, this master could catch "a little girl's shadow reflected in a pool of water" with his bare hands. He apparently was a descendent of the Schlemiel natives who would snatch up and devour any kind of shadow. He worked for a casket maker removing shadows from the deceased so no shadows got inside the casket. Old Man Thumbs the Casket Maker has always quipped, "I make caskets for people who are a mere shadow of their former selves, not for the shadows themselves." Thus, the Master Shadow Catcher was employed there.

"If he is a master, then . . ." thought Alice. "I just know he'll catch that impostor shadow for me."

Alice straddled her bicycle and set out through the moonlit town to visit Old Man Thumbs the Casket Maker. Alice peddled along the streets; her bicycle with one shadow and Alice with two shadows reflected in the moonlight.

> I inadvertently added a beard to my portrait,
> so I grew a real beard.
>
> I inadvertently hired a gatekeeper,
> so I built myself a real gate.
>
> I inadvertently got two shadows in the moonlight,
> so I set out two real moons.

This was the song the "ruodabuort" (the backward troubadour) sang as he played the accordion. But Alice knew. She knew that it takes more than just cardboard, string, and scissors to raise up two moons.

How to Find a Child Without a Shadow

"The solution to duplicate shadows is," said Dr. Conclusion, "to make you become two Alices." How was she to become two Alices? Dr. Conclusion was not willing to hazard a guess.

Poor Alice rode her bicycle about for three days, and at long last located Old Man Thumbs the Casket Maker. But the Master was not there. Word was that the shadows he had removed were terribly wrinkled, so he had taken them to the dry cleaners to have them pressed. No one had seen him since. Alice didn't know what to do. How was she to unify these two shadows she had?

Possible solutions to the problem:

1. Cut off the legs of one shadow with a sharp saw, fold them up and return them to the Shadow Shop.

2. Have the two shadows discuss the matter, and have one of them go away. If that doesn't work, then they take turns being the shadow on alternate days.

3. Have everything, have two shadows (draw the second shadow on the carpet in black paint).

4. Brag about having two shadows to everyone, and convince yourself that you are happy about it.

5. Make sure that your shadow overlaps with someone else's shadow at all times so no one will notice you have two.

"Which one do you think is the best choice?" Alice wrote. Circle the one you think is best, cut out this page and send it to me. Yet, even if she had taken any of this advice, there was no guarantee that the problem would be solved. Smokey the cat had this to say.

"Surely somewhere in the world is a child without a shadow, so all you have to do is find that child and make friends. Between the child without a shadow and Alice who has two, they would have two shadows—which would be just right."

To the Beginning Of Shadowland

"Is she asleep?" said Alice's shadow.

"She seems to be," answered Alice's other shadow.

Alice's shadow furtively peered into Alice's sleeping face. Hugging Smokey and her stuffed egg doll, she was sound asleep with an innocent expression on her face.

"About that terrifying snail . . ." said Alice's shadow.

"Yes, about that terrifying snail," replied Alice's other shadow.

"It seems that it gets into the shadows of livestock and dolls and sucks the blood out. The shadows remain as they are, but the livestock and dolls become anemic, lose weight, and eventually die."

"The Mollos-dog,[1] the green-haired boy doll, the wind-up mother, the unpainted weather vane, and the King of the Dachshunds who wears galoshes . . ."

"It got all of them."

"Yes, it got all of them," said Alice's shadow.

"We've got to make sure that we stay clean and that nothing contaminating gets inside us." Alice's other shadow took a small broom and began to sweep away its own dust.

"We should probably be on our way soon," said Alice's shadow. "Shall we be on our way now?"

"I've heard about shadows who detach themselves from the real thing and go on walks in the dead of night."

"How about to Shadowland?"

"Let's bring Alice with us, as we discussed."

The two shadows held hands and began walking, and the sleeping Alice, in her pajamas, rose up like a somnambulant.

"We are on our way," said Alice's shadow. "To Shadowland."

Alice, with her eyes still closed, had no idea yet where she was being taken.

"When we get to Shadowland, we will solve the mysteries

1. A dog bred to be a livestock guardian dog.

of why you have two shadows, of the one poor colored pencil that was sewn up in light, of 'anyway,' and 'for the time being,' and 'also,' and 'then,' and all the other mysteries as well."

Do you want to know where Alice and her two shadows went?

Stand a pencil vertically before you. Walk ninety-nine paces in the direction the pencil's shadow lies. Close your eyes. If there is a door there, knock. That will be the entrance to Shadowland.

ALICE IN BOOKLAND

The Cutout Old Woman

The scissors, by all appearances, were no different from regular scissors. Alice had thought perhaps she had been swindled by the man at the antique shop. This was because he hadn't given her any change. Alice had intended to use the change from her purchase of the scissors to buy biscuits for her cat Smokey on the way home. She had asked the antique dealer for the change, but he had told her he didn't owe her any.

Startled, Alice said, "You mean to tell me that these rusty old scissors are that expensive?"

But the man replied, "These aren't just any scissors."

He took the scissors from Alice. "Watch this," he said, and with a devious, bug-eyed glance, rather like The Sandman,[2] he picked up the picture book which lay beside him. It was a book about birds which had been on the shelf unsold for seven months already. On the cover, printed off center, was a pen and ink drawing of a bull-headed shrike.

The man looked long and hard at the bull-headed shrike on the cover, and then deliberately proceeded to cut it out. When the pen and ink bird had been partially cut out, it began to flap its wings. When it was finally released, it called

---

2. Reference to E.T.A. Hoffman's short story *Der Sandmann* (1816), which revolves around the mythical figure of the Sandman who was said to steal children's eyes and eat them.

out with a harsh crackle and flew out of the antique shop into the blue sky above.

"What do you think of that?" the man said with a self-congratulatory air. "Whatever is cut out with these scissors comes to life."

Alice decided to buy the scissors on the spot.

At home, Alice sat down on her bed and called out, "Smokey! Look at the incredible scissors I just bought. See? I'll make you some buddies."

This was going to be Alice's reward to Smokey for learning how to fold his forepaws so nicely.

At first, Smokey was afraid of Alice's scissors and ran under the bed. But as soon as he realized they weren't for cutting off his whiskers, he relaxed and approached her.

Alice opened a picture book called *Cats*, and happily began cutting out some of the cats pictured there. One, two, three, four . . . before she knew it, the room was full of cats. All of the cutout cats cried meow, meow in English, just like Smokey.

"There. Now you're not all alone anymore, Smokey," said Alice. "Now, you won't need to get hysterical when the moon is out at night, and you won't need to jump up and down all over my violin."

The cutout cats gathered around Smokey's milk dish and began greedily lapping up the milk.

One unfortunate thing was that though the cutout cats were the same as Smokey on the front side, they had English printed on the reverse side. (It was probably the author's explanation on the back of each cat illustration.)

The next day, Alice decided to cut out a solitary old woman who appeared on the last page of a picture book. Smokey wasn't paying any attention to her anymore because he had so many friends now. So, it occurred to her that she could cut out the old woman and make friends with her. Judging from appearance, the old woman didn't seem to be overly garrulous, nor was she riding a broom, so Alice thought it was safe.

Alice began to cut out the old woman, using the scissors skillfully, but cutting out her silhouette turned out to be more difficult than Alice had anticipated because the pen and ink crone was so delicately drawn.

In the meantime, the cats' milk had come to a boil and was bubbling fiercely, which distracted Alice. Her hand slipped and she cut the old woman's nose right off.

"Oh, I'm so sorry!" cried Alice, alarmed. She tried gluing the nose back on, and then she tried taping it back in place, but nothing seemed to work. She ended up with a nose-less cutout.

What happened to the nose that got cut off, you ask? It lay in the palm of Alice's hand pitifully sniffing around for something, but then finally went who-knows-where. I will save the story of the faceless nose and its wild wanderings for another day.

The cutout old woman spoke up. "Alice, you got into this fix because you insist on cutting out nothing but pictures. Cut out words! Words, I tell you. You can only bring to life what is visible with a picture, but with words you can delight in the anticipation of what wonderful thing might jump out at you." Put that way, Alice thought the old woman was absolutely right. As an experiment, Alice took the book of fairy tales lying next to her and set her scissors to the first two lines of this song.

If a horse were a wish,
A vagabond would ride it.
If a turnip were a watch,
I'd wear it at my waist.

At that moment, a vagabond mounted on a horse appeared from among the pages of the book.

"Thanks!" he said, waved to Alice and off he went into the distance.

Then, Alice proceeded to cut out the two-syllable word "turnip" with great care (and a touch of spite). Suddenly, a large, bright red turnip came rolling out of the small book. Next Alice cut out the word "watch." The same thing happened. The book began to vibrate with a rhythmic beat, tick-tock, tick-tock, and out from the pages slid a shiny new pocket watch.

"It is much fancier than the pocket watch that belonged to my uncle who passed away," said Alice. But the old woman looked askance at her. The poem suggested that a turnip and a pocket watch are equivalent, but that the pocket watch doesn't exist. Despite this, greedy Alice got her hands on both the turnip and the pocket watch. This stirred some considerable dissatisfaction in the old woman. Alice became more and more engrossed and proceeded to cut out a great variety of words. Compass, a button made from a Mollos-dog's tooth, a green-haired boy doll, a wind-up mother, an unpainted weathervane, the Pied Piper, a paper moon, a lace calendar—Alice's room filled with all these things that had come back to life.

"Look at all this! What fun!" Brandishing the scissors, Alice stood enthralled. Smokey the cat leapt over the book

Alice had been cutting, and though he felt a touch of jealousy, he joined her in cavorting about.

The problem came after this. While she was cutting out all those words, she became curious about the word "love," and made the mistake of cutting it out too.

Of course, Alice was fascinated as she had never seen what "love" looked like. But perhaps she was also being contrary and wanted to give the scissors, which had the power to bring things back to life, a hard time.

The scissors slowly cut out the word "love."

When the cut was complete, Alice suddenly cried out, "Oh!" and lost consciousness.

The reader, now, must continue this sad story of Alice and the cutouts. In what form do you think the word "love" emerged?

1. A strange monster (like King Kong).
2. Nothing came out at all.
3. A red apple rolled out.
4. One wisp of smoke floated up.
5. It remained as the word "love."

Write your choice on the last page of your notebook.

Alice Fell In Love with an Eraser

Yes. Alice, fell in love with an eraser and wrote this poem.

> An eraser can erase anything.
> It can rub out
> the chatterbox honey bee
> and Humpty Dumpty.
> It can even rub out the vigilant moon
> so as to bring darkness upon the

night when Alice and her cat Smokey go
to the garden next door
to steal rushes.

It can erase
anything that Alice detests.
It rubs out March, July and September,
The 7th, the 11th and the 23rd,
and any other dates.
The eraser transforms
everything into memories,
with its magical powers.

Write "Alice" and erase it,
and Alice herself will vanish from
this world.
The eraser sometimes
acts the murderer as well.

But write "Alice"
in that blank space again.
Erase it.
Write Alice again.
Erase it again.
Write Alice again.
Erase it.
Write it.

Alice can be there in
perpetuity,
but the eraser wears away
and eventually disappears.

What is sorrowful for the eraser

is that it only makes things vanish,
so more and more is lost.
Nothing is ever gained.

The eraser rubbed out the last six beautiful lines of this poem. What were those lines? Alice could not remember no matter how hard she tried. Would you think up some for her?

It is possible, for anyone, to have memories of things that never really happened.

Que Sera Sera

The French writer Pierre Cami's[1] short stories often feature a secondary character, a man whose jaw is tied up with a red bandage. Cami does not explain why a red bandage, but I can't help but chuckle as I imagine some idiot burdened with a long, long *ago*.[2]

Perhaps this man was a singularly timid person who had no particularly distinguishing characteristics that would make him stand out.

Yet, perhaps it was a time when suits and neckties were being mass produced. Perhaps people lived in high-rise apartment buildings, read mass produced newspapers, chewed mass produced bread, commuted in their mass produced cars to huge corporations. Perhaps they all were on the verge of becoming completely identical.

(The following is Longlongago's journal, which is a product of my spontaneous thoughts. That said, don't think this is a modern-day social satire. Ultimately, it is a farce about a time "long-long-ago".)

---

1. Pierre Henri Cami (1884–1958), a French humorist.

2. Terayama makes a bilingual play on words: *ago* means chin or jaw, and is also the English spelling in the expression Long, long ago. The pun can be understood as "long, long ago in a far away land . . ." or as "long, long chin" which needs to be bound up by a bandage.

Day One

Hanako, the co-ed who was researching the existence of dolphins, came to visit. She had completed about half of her senior thesis on whether or not dolphins are present 10,000 meters beneath the surface of the ocean. After we had chatted a little in my apartment, she said suddenly, "I saw you in town today."

But I hadn't been in town. I told her she was mistaken, but she insisted that she had not mistaken someone else for me. She was sure she had seen me.

Day Two

The air was heavy today, so I holed up in my apartment, until Hanao, the unshaven football player, came over in the evening and said, "Hey, you're home already? I just saw you in town. How can that be?" "There must be some misunderstanding," I said. "I didn't even set foot out of the apartment today."

Hanao snorted, "You don't have to be shy about it. I won't think any the worse of you. Going to the aquarium to see the crabs is nothing to be ashamed of. As a matter of fact, I go there myself on occasion."

Day Three

It is hard to dissuade someone from their misapprehensions. Despite the fact that I had been in my apartment, both Hanako and Hanao said they had seen "me" elsewhere. They insisted that they had seen me in two different locations, though I hadn't gone to either place.

I secured the apartment door from the outside (so I could not escape confinement without help) and sat with my legs tucked under me holding my breath, but when Hanako and Hanao came over that evening, they simply laughed dismissively at me. They both spoke frankly like two linked wieners.

"I saw you in town on the train today."

I stood up indignantly and slammed the table with nearly enough force to break it in half. "What the hell are you talking about? I went nowhere. I was in my apartment all day." But Hanako and Hanao just snickered and peered back at me.

"I'll get a lawyer!" I shouted.

Strangely enough, Hanako said, "Yes, a lawyer might be necessary. It is a crime to grope young ladies in a crowded train, you know."

I began to get confused and started to hate the "me" they were talking about. What were they telling me that I had done?

Day Four

Well, I decided to slip out and go find "me" in town. I tied a red bandage around my chin so I would not be mistaken for anyone else, waited for dark and then went out. I searched everywhere that Hanako and Hanao had said they saw "me." I even checked the homeless people under the underpass and peeked into manholes.

But I did not find even a single man who resembled "me" in town. Exhausted and a little shaky from the search, I made my way home and climbed the stairs to my apartment.

But when I got there, I heard people talking inside. (No one was supposed to be in my apartment so it stands to reason that I was astonished by what I saw.)

There was no mistaking it, Hanako was talking to "me" in there! Hanako was telling "me" that she saw me in town and was laughing about the red bandage around my chin. The "me" in there, looking incredulous, was completely enthralled by her explanation.

Then it came to me in an instant as I stood outside the door.

"If that is 'me,' then who the hell am I?"

24,000 KISSES

The first kiss was when you were only seventeen and I was nineteen. It was where the lilacs bloom in the cemetery, and the kiss tasted vaguely of fish.

The fifth kiss was when you were a freshman in college. I was passionate about yacht design. Behind the library where the skylark sings, our kiss burned ardently.

I am a gang member. I don't shave yet. My name is not in the who's who of Japanese gentlemen. But I loved you so very, very much.

The 100th kiss was right after you graduated. I had just gotten out of the boys reform school. The ocean reflected in the cherry blossom dish, and the kiss tasted like a wild animal.

The 1,000th kiss was when you were a teaching assistant at the Western Dressmaking Institute. I was planning a big bank heist. Under the great elm tree, the kiss was as shy as a squirrel.

The 1,001st kiss was still when you were a teaching assistant at the Western Dressmaking Institute. The bank heist had been unsuccessful and I was in jail. Through the screen between us in the visitation room, the kiss tasted like a rusty nail.

The 9,000th kiss was when you had become another man's wife. I was a kingpin in the underworld. We met unexpectedly at a summer resort and the kiss was moist as a flower.

The 10,012th kiss was when you became a nun. I committed fraud and was on the lam. The kiss, surprising and unexpected, made my heart bound like a fawn's.

I am a gang member. I still don't shave. I have twelve previous convictions, and I migrate from south to north like a swallow. I am still in love with you, but they tell me that you have already gone through the change of life.

The 20,000th kiss was when you were in the convalescent home suffering from intestinal catarrh. I tucked a fenced imitation diamond necklace in my shirt and traveled a long, long way to see you. The kiss, on that convalescent bed, was like a shriveled apricot.

The record player plays the tune "24,000 kisses" gaily. But the lyrics sound so false. You see, I was only able to kiss you 23,999 times.

The 23,999th kiss was when you were already in your grave. I gnashed my dentures and wept in the cemetery where the lilacs bloom, and the kiss tasted vaguely of fish.

Love lasts forever.

Tap, tap, tap. The sound of them making my casket reverberates into the air. I am broken-hearted. It can take a lifetime to have 23,999 kisses, but 10,000 nights would be too short for that final 24,000th kiss.

I loved you from the bottom of my heart. Can you hear me? I quietly wipe my mouth. No use having moist lips when you are about to take your own life.

THE THIEF'S TANGO

Norio, his back up against the wall, breathed raggedly. Why does that swan have black wings, I wonder?

The swan, which he reached out his hand to steal, suddenly appeared to have black wings when it flapped them. That he spoiled his chance to abscond with it made his frustration at being betrayed even greater.

When he opened his eyes, the ball had already begun. The dancers were flowing and mingling together like wind-blown newspapers. Norio looked at a long shadow on the large ballroom floor. A single bright red rose rolled seemingly from nowhere onto his shadow. When he bent to pick it up, something suddenly held his hand down.

"Young thief. Won't you dance the tango with me?"

Startled, Norio withdrew his hand. There stood a madam with a beauty mark. "I can't dance. I'm a wall flower."

The baron narrowed his eyes and stroked the wings of the black bird. If the baron said, "Wings, black bird!" the black bird would flap its wings with ease. When the swan flapped its wings, they were blacker than any black bird alive.

It is complete.

The baron drew open the curtains of his studio. Night spread all through the spacious room. The baron lit a cigarette. He was a solitary man. He did not recognize the true essence or definition of anything or anyone. He abhorred the societal convention, practiced only for the sake of maintaining harmony, of dividing things up into their own dominions: e.g. thieves stealing, roses blooming, birds flying.

His interest lay in creating counterfeits. With considerable ease he plagiarized poetry, dealt in phony Michelangelos as well as fake jewels, not to mention fraudulent murders. The delight of finally creating a fabricated black bird which was a dead ringer for the imperial swan kept in a museum was his "greatest triumph of all time," to borrow the much repeated expression from the servant crow.

"Here we are, dear." The madam turned to Norio and smiled as she closed the door behind her. Exhausted from dancing, Norio stood bashfully, his arms hanging loosely at his sides. When the madam went to take a shower, Norio fell onto the couch, and then heard a voice.

"Joey, wipe me down, will you?" Then, a leopard, born in Ivory Coast came sleekly in from the adjacent room. And suddenly began to lick the dripping wet madam almost as if it were attacking her. The leopard's tongue was the madam's towel.

The madam closed her eyes with pleasure and said, "there are tomatoes and some beef in the refrigerator." Norio had become quite sleepy. The madam turned her beautifully fleshed out body to Norio and encouraged him. "Well, well, my little gigolo. I am not going to let you sleep tonight." When the baron looked at the newspaper first thing in the morning, he couldn't but think that what he saw was a mistake. But upon review, he found it was not so.

Death of the Swan. Due to unseasonably low temperatures last night, the treasured Imperial Swan died despite all efforts to save it.

The baron folded up the newspaper in a foul temper. The most disappointing moment for a counterfeiter is when the authentic item loses its value. Obviously, a fake loses its worth when the real thing dies. The baron pressed the buzzer and the servant crow appeared.

"Will you be going out, sir?"

"I'm going to take a walk."

What an odd town, Norio thought to himself as he looked down from the window on the town the madam had ventured out into. It was almost as if good fortune had come to rest pinned up on this sunny town like a butterfly pinned up on a wall. The air had become too heavy, surely that was it. It's been one strange thing after another. For instance, even though various fruits had ripened, there were no windfalls. Smoke hung still in the blue sky, and if you were paying attention, you saw that the flower girl, the delinquent boy and the sailor were all walking the straight and narrow. It was as if they walked straight ahead determining their respective domains by the grooves in the concrete.

The air is too heavy, I am sure of it. No one notices it even though that is what is to blame for all this.

Norio chuckled. I suppose they will all be crushed eventually by the heaviness of the air. Then, grasping the risks of the circumstances, he slurped down shrimp soup for breakfast with oceanic gusto and thought, how free I am!

With that he, not knowing what to do with so much freedom, felt mildly ill. Norio moved away from the window and called the leopard. "Joey! Shall we play a game?"

Almost as if he were the only person walking along haphazardly zigzagging through the dense air of the strange town, the baron dealt out playing cards. After dealing, he faced the three Indians and gave them several cards for the ones they threw. The baron and these three Indians were regulars at the café called Dizzyland. He was a bit thirsty as he dealt.

All three Indians spoke together, "Full house!"

"Straight flush," said the baron, expressionless as he pulled the poker chips toward himself.

"It's hot."

We get it. We lost because it's hot, thought the Indians. The street below was visible through the open window. The madam with the beauty mark just happened to be passing by. She rounded the corner with a swing of her supple hips. The baron stood up suddenly.

"I'll collect my winnings later."

When the breeze came in, the baron was no longer in the room. Thick rays of sun threaded through the straw weave of the panama hat he had forgotten on his way out. The three Indians looked at each other recalling the red flower which never knew Kansas.

"That's not fair. Not fair, I tell you."

Norio twisted and squirmed ticklishly. The leopard, Joey, was a female. Norio, now naked and perspiring, attempted to escape. The leopard was incredibly gentle. Their ragged breath colliding, Joey and Norio writhed entangled on the bed. Mari the maid, who had hurriedly come in, stood blushing and speechless.

After several tries, Mari finally managed to say, "Uh, excuse me, . . ." Norio peered out from under the sheets and looked her way.

"Good Lord! You can't just barge in like this!" Mari stood uneasily not knowing what to do. Mari had taken a shine to

Norio from the moment she saw him the night before. But she had something even more important to say now.

"The missus has run away."

The baron had stashed the madam in a suitcase and was walking along the river. He did not know whether he had fallen in love with her or whether he wanted to make a replica of her. He gazed at his reflection in the river absentmindedly and switched the suitcase to the other hand suddenly as if he had just had a revelation.

"That's it. What a good idea."

The baron's reflection still remained on the river for a time after he set off. The reflection looked defiant in a lonesome way, and presently disappeared. It was clear that he had fallen in love.

"The baron?" Norio threw back the sheets. Joey, embarrassed, burrowed back under. "I'll go see about it, then."

"But you can't go like that . . ." Mari hesitated. Norio then realized that he was stark naked. He showered and got dressed. He gulped down the last mouthful of soup and flew out the door, not bothering to close it behind him. It was, however, not long before he came back.

"I will bring her back no matter what! I broke into the baron's house just last night." The baron put the key in the keyhole and let out a sigh. He maintained that love is something one steals. He laid the madam on the bed and lit a cigar. He was bound and determined to create a replica of her.

I must be a descendent of the gods, he thought to himself. I am able to accomplish anything I conceive of, and without feeling the burden of free choice.

It was plausible that he was god-like in that he was never troubled by conscience in the least whether he committed murder or created a replica of someone. If I am in no way conscious of sin, then I am even capable of flying.

The baron looked down on the madam with an intense and concentrated gaze. Her elegant leg, with a sheen of perspiration, protruded from her robe. He was about to kiss her when he heard the voice of the servant crow.

"Someone's at the door."

"I have come to see the baron."

"He's not here."

"Liar. I saw him come in." Norio was breathing hard and appeared to be about ready to attack the crow.

"That young buck can just come into the mirror chamber," said the baron to the servant crow. The mirror chamber was one of the baron's masterpieces; a room with all the walls made entirely of mirrors.

The chamber was such that once you set foot inside, you could no longer distinguish between your reflections and your real self, and you simply disappeared.

From the time the replica-fanatic baron created this space, there is no telling how many people had been drawn into the mirrors and lost themselves there. Every time it happened, the baron would laugh aloud.

They only distinguished themselves from others by their features or clothing. So, when they were surrounded by others who had the same features and clothing, instantly they no longer knew who they were themselves.

When Norio opened the door, he stood stock-still and drew in his breath sharply.

There were seven Norios looking at him with the same expression. The baron was in a foul mood because his romantic intentions had been interrupted. He tore off the madam's robe roughly and forced her into submission. It got to the point where the madam could only gasp like a fish out of water. She lay there looking at the baron emotionless, giving no response to his kisses.

"This is always the way it turns out for me," the baron said sadly, showing the despondency of a victor.

"You think you can do anything, but you are sorely mistaken," said the madam.

"But I can do anything. I am capable of anything."

"You can't fly. You can't fly like a bird." "Across the sky?"

"Yes, across the sky."

He tossed away his cigar and narrowed his eyes as he looked up at the smoke stack. Norio clicked his tongue peevishly. Yet, it might have been one of the Norios in the mirrors who tisk-tisked. The sound alone reached Norio's ears with an empty ring. Which one am I really?!

The real person is the one who is watching. But the Norio who was looking at the reflected Norio was actually the one who was being watched. I might be one of the mirror images. Perhaps all the Norios will disappear completely by looking at each other. Norio exhaled like a wild animal and turned to the mirrors.

I am a thief. If I am a real thief, then I must make off with myself.

At the very same moment, the baron stood on the top of the smoke stack, shirt-less in just his briefs humming to himself.

So, here I go: I'll fly like a bird and be as free as a god. As he brought to mind Otto Lilienthal's *Birdflight as the Basis of*

Aviation[1] he spread his arms like wings and began to flap as he threw himself into the air.

I've got it! Norio shouted out suddenly. You can't look! You are watched because you watch the others. He faced the mirrors and closed his eyes.

I shut my eyes and feel my body: my hands, my chest . . . this is me! If I just don't look, then I can feel my own actual body. The laying on of hands is incontrovertible proof that I am alive.

Then with his eyes still closed, he threw himself with all his might against the mirrors. With a resounding crash the mirrors shattered.

He fell!

The baron, the bird who could not fly, fell head first through the fissure in the sky of the cloudy mirrors. He did not resurface again.

Presently, Norio opened his eyes and he saw the blue sky before him. He was pierced by broken shards of glass, but shouted, Here I am! This is me! I finally, at long last, stole myself.

Color rose gently to his cheeks, and he gradually lost consciousness in the dazzling blue sky as if falling asleep.

The madam, startled, sat up in bed and whispered, "What was that sound?" Glancing down and realizing that she had been stripped, she suddenly became embarrassed. Why was she here in this place and what was this large stuffed animal doing here? With that, those great black wings began to beat wildly. The swan. This is where it all begins.

1. Otto Lilienthal was a German aviator who is said to be the first man to achieve human flight successfully. He published *Birdflight as the Basis of Aviation* in 1889.

JOKER JOE

One

Joker Joe was a heartbroken fellow. He was a man who had died once, made it as far as the gates of hell, and then returned. There was a reason he could not yet face death.

When he got drunk, alone at the bar called Domino, he sang Yves Montand's[2] chansons in a rough gravelly voice.

> The donkey, the king, and I
> will all die tomorrow
> The donkey of starvation,
> The king of boredom,
> And I of love.
> The month is May.

This was the song that expressed what was in Joker Joe's heart. Joker Joe was a man who died for love, and then, was revived by it.

> Et moi d'amour
> Au mois de mai[3]

Two

Once there was a composer. The brazen Jack of Diamonds, who did nothing but play the piano from morning into the

2. Yves Montand (1921–1991) was a French singer and actor.
3. And I of love. The month is May.

wee hours. A descendent of the villainous Bascoms, he was a licentious man, sporting a loathsome mustache. On top of all this, the music he composed was exclusively for funerals.

The young chimney sweep asked, "Why do you only make funeral music?"

"But I like funeral music," he replied, looking at the boy with eyes deeply obsessed with death. The boy ran away terrified. Only gloomy strains could be heard from the Jack of Diamond's attic. Sometimes the old couple who ran Speed, the bar directly beneath him, complained.

"He's ruining us with all that depressing music."

"I should say so. No one wants to have a few drinks serenaded by funeral music?" "Can't he do something a little more . . ."

"Couldn't he compose music a little more cheerful?"

The crow, perched on the top of the saké cask, said *sotto voce*, "God, I am so sick of funeral music."

Three

One person had feelings for the Jack of Diamonds, and that was Mizue, the sweet and gentle flower vendor girl of the town.

Mizue maintained that the Jack of Diamonds wrote nothing but dark music because he was cursed.

"If only he could sell his music somehow. If he could, then he would become famous and wealthy. Then I am sure he would write more cheerful music."

It was around this time that Mizue consulted a private detective. "What do we have to do to make his music sell?"

The detective, a fat man who owned a dachshund, said, "That's easy. The only place funeral music is going to be played is at a funeral, so all you need to do is to canvas the funeral homes and ask if they need funeral music."

Four

So, Mizue went all around the town on sales calls to funeral homes asking if they needed funeral music.

"Funeral music?" the gravedigger asked back; to which Mizue sang Ives Montand's chanson.

> The dead leaves collected with the shovel.
> You see, I did not forget . . .
> The dead leaves collected with the shovel,
> The memories and the regrets . . .

"You see, for example, this is just one version of a funeral dirge," she explained. "In other words, these pieces make funeral services more enjoyable." Mizue, her hair festooned with flowers, spoke in words that resonated deeply with most of the funeral directors. They chimed in saying, "Absolutely" or "Most certainly," but not one of them bought a single song. This was because not a soul had died in the last month and thus there had been no funerals.

Five

"So, you can't sell any funeral music because there haven't been any funerals, you say?" said the monk on the chessboard. "All you have to do is arrange for a funeral, right?" "But . . ." Mizue began hesitantly.

"You can't have a funeral if no one has died." Then an evil smile came over the monk's face and he said, "I'll introduce you to an excellent assassin, then. The assassin kills someone. If someone dies then there will be a funeral service. If there is a funeral service, they'll need a funeral dirge. Then everything will end happily ever after, right?"

A feeling of terror came over Mizue. Yet, as she thought of the Jack of Diamonds and the deeply melancholy funeral dirges he was writing, she felt she had no other alternative. She asked to be introduced to the assassin.

Four different flowers. Four assassins.

As it happened, all the assassins showed up: the Rose, the Tulip, the Lilac and the Amaryllis. One of them flashed a blood-covered jack knife and said, "You get a fifty percent discount if this is a crime of passion."

Six

But Mizue was a gentle-hearted girl. She could not bring herself to cause a murder for the sake of one paltry song. After much thought, she decided to ask Joker Joe. Weeping, she begged good-natured Joker Joe, who listened nodding all the while. He finally said, "I see . . . I see. You want me to pretend I'm dead tomorrow, right? Fair enough. For your sake, Mizue, I will pretend to be dead. It's nothing. I am the fifty-third card in the deck, useless and unwanted. If I can be of assistance, I am ready to die at a moment's notice."

So, Joker Joe "died" for her and Mizue put him in an aphrodisiac infused casket. Then she dashed back to the home of the Jack of Diamonds. "I sold one of your funeral songs! We finally made some money from your music."

The Jack of Diamonds was overjoyed and hugged Mizue ardently. A smile playing on his mustached lip, he said, "Well done. After the funeral I'll make you my wife!"

Seven

Joker Joe was devastated when he heard this, for the truth was, he was in love with Mizue. He had wanted to make Mizue happy by feigning death. But from his hiding place in the casket, he found it unbearable to see Mizue and the Jack of Diamonds gazing fondly at each other, the funeral music in the background.

Mizue did not know that the Jack of Diamonds already had a wife and was an uncommon master of chicanery. Joker Joe knew he had to save Mizue at all costs. Yet, the preparations for the funeral proceeded quickly, and everyone in the town spoke of the much anticipated funeral music.

Joker Joe thought to himself. "What do I have to do to save Mizue and not interrupt the funeral? I've got it! There is only one thing to do," he said slapping his knee. It was a serene May day.

Eight

The Jack of Diamonds was practicing his funeral piece when a man in mourning dress and a kerchief on his head approached. He produced a book, and with mock sincerity said, "I wish to make a gift of this book to you, rare among the rare and quintessentially unique."

"Really! What kind of book is it?" the Jack of Diamonds asked as he looked at the man with great interest.

"It is a book of the basest interest, a pornographic work depicting the bedroom of a despicably obscene king," the man said. It was at this moment when the Jack of Diamonds revealed his true nature. "This is just this kind of book I have been waiting for!" He grabbed the book away from the man as he said this, and instantly began leafing through the pages.

Yet, he got nowhere as the pages were all stuck together. So he resorted to licking his finger in an attempt to flip to the first page. When he did, however, it was blank. He tried again with the second and third pages, licking his finger and turning the pages, but still he found nothing was written on any of them.

"What the hell is this? There isn't anything good in here at all!" shouted the Jack of Diamonds. "Look further! Look further!" exclaimed the man in mourning.

So the Jack of Diamonds kept on licking his finger and turning page after page finding nothing—and then it began to circulate through his system: the book had been rigged with a lethal substance. The Jack of Diamonds began to convulse, shouting, "I've been poisoned!"

Just then, the man in mourning suddenly shed his disguise. It was Joker Joe. He said, "Now I can enjoy your funeral dirge to my heart's content . . . at your funeral."

Nine

But, Mizue hated Joker Joe for this. His actions on her behalf, which emanated from his love for her, were only received as those of a jealous murderer. In the end, Joker Joe was the only one ever to be banished from the town of Playingcards, and he became an outcast. As the fifty-third card in the deck, he wandered and sang of his unrequited love for Mizue well into his old age.

> The donkey, the king and I
> Will all die tomorrow.
> The donkey of starvation,
> The king of boredom,
> And I of love.
> The month is May.

FLAME

The middle school boy had finally snuck away to a secluded shed and tried to light a cigarette, but couldn't get the match to light. Two matches, three matches; he tried nearly a dozen times, but all his efforts were in vain. What was the matter? He held the box of matches up to the light shining through the window like shafts of straw and thought. He desperately longed for the bitterness of tears from choking on cigarette smoke.

Even after drying them in the sun, the matches were useless. For some unknown reason this odd curiosity was happening all over the town the next morning.

The blacksmith, sleepy-eyed, could not get a fire going with his bellows, so he called to the fat old lady next door thinking there was some kind of mishap. But the phenomenon had already occurred at her house too.

"I can't get anything to light in my house either," the fat old lady shouted back in her piercing voice. "I can't get anything to light no matter what I do."

Something terrible has happened.

A rooster fluttered about.

A young girl opened her window early in the morning, faced the volcano as always and yawned slightly, but suddenly her expression changed and she whispered, "The fire in the volcano is out."

Fire had extinguished itself completely from the town.

Mao was a homeless waif. He lived in the woods with the birds inside a hollow in the biggest elm tree in the forest. No one in the town knew anything about Mao other than that he often sang a strange song called "Everything Has Disappeared."

> Everything has disappeared
> Neither seed nor crumb remain
> No sky for birds
> No wind for wings
> For we have stopped singing

"This isn't working either. Just as I thought," said the cooking instructor holding a large lens over the ground. All the townspeople looked anxiously into the face of the mayor.

I see. That didn't work either.

The mayor, despondent, turned his eyes to the heavens. The sky extended infinitely upward, and the nearly unbearable sunlight shone directly down on them. Yet, the lens would not generate a flame even with concentrated sunlight.

"Damn you lens! Pretending to be blind," murmured the cooking instructor. "Who stole our fire?"

"Life without fire is hell."

"How are we supposed to go on without fire?"

Everyone began to fret agitatedly. Even the blacksmith walked about nervously, his hands clasped before him.

Those bellows couldn't possibly betray me . . .

In the most remote restaurant in town, the scullery maid Yumi thought about the fire uproar as she washed dishes in the back corner of the kitchen.

"Maybe this town had no spark from the very beginning."

She finished the dishes, and since the restaurant was closed for the day due to the fire ruckus, she decided to go to her boyfriend Mao whom she hadn't seen for a while.

She thought that he would be the only one who would agree with her new theory that the town never had any spark to begin with. But as soon as he saw Yumi, Mao pressed his lips to hers, and she lost the presence of mind to tell him. They drank greedily of each other as a fawn drinks greedily from a pool of water. They both closed their eyes and in that darkness imagined the other's face reflected in a mirror. After an hour of long silence and dreams, Mao opened the curtains in the hotel room and looked down on the town square. Yumi joined him at the window, and nestled into Mao's chest.

In the town square, it just so happened that there were two gigantic stones being hauled there in a cart. The burro brayed. The townspeople surrounded them with anticipation and anxiety.

The blacksmith and the ex-boxer bodyguard had been chosen. The blacksmith lifted one stone mightily and threw it down so as to strike the other. The stones violently collided and generated a small intense spark. It sounded something like the call of a pheasant.

"There wasn't any spark to begin with, you know," Yumi told Mao, almost as if she were singing. A woodland swallowtail butterfly flew out through the window.

"Everyone was using fire routinely. They all took it for granted. You only realize the true meaning of fire when you have lost it. You see true flames once you have sparked them yourself."

A cheer arose in the town square. The women, straw and matches in hand, all rushed to get a bit of spark from the flints. The square was teeming with a herd of women, when the mayor shouted, "This is our fire! From now on I want you all to strike stone on stone and make your own spark. We will return to a earlier time. We will return to ancient times when matches and lighters had not been invented yet."

The ex-boxer caught on quickly and struck the gigantic stones together again. Sparks flew up into the blue sky and went out. Everyone stood in deep awe of the heat emanating from those bright sparks.

"The meaning of fire has been brought back to life for the first time in this town," said Yumi feverishly.

"Finally, everyone will remember their roles in life. It is a pity, though, that all those things we take for granted, not just fire, will disappear suddenly one day. There are so many things that we all have forgotten unconsciously, yet they touch our lives every day. Even love, don't you think?"

Yumi spoke to Mao turning her cheek to the wind, which blew as though caressing the elm leaves.

"But now . . ." But now . . .

A chick was about to hatch in the nest that floated on the flowing river.

> Everything has disappeared
> Neither seed nor crumb remain
> No sky for birds
> No wind for wings
> For we have stopped singing

However, it was nothing more than a fleeting moment during which the lack of fire seemed to invite a spring-like season. Then presently, a rogue season visited the town. It came in the form of a rotund executioner who donned a black waistcoat. When an execution took place in the town, he always turned to the condemned person and pronounced, "I'll try to make this as bloodless as possible." Then with deep sympathy he would give that person a sharp look, as if to say that his compensation was inappropriately low.

This man took it into his head one day to try to turn a quick profit. He thought, we don't have to use those inconvenient flints when all I have to do is go get fire from the neighboring village. That's it. If I do that, then I won't have to earn my keep by being showered with the blood of those prisoners reeking of iron. I'll see the mayor and make the deal, thought the executioner as he shaved. When Yumi heard about this, she feared the worst.

Yumi shook awake the sleeping Mao who was nestled into the elm tree hollow with the birds, and told him what she'd heard.

Mao shook his head repeatedly as he listened to her report. We can't let this happen. We have to nip this one in the bud, he said. He knew that if fire was brought from the next village, the street lamps, the sails, and the volcano would all be restored to brightness. At the very least, it was certain that a mote of good fortune would return to the hands of the villagers.

But, we have to fight this small bit of good fortune. In order to know the meaning of fire, one must extinguish a thousand fires.

I have to stop the executioner from bringing it here, thought Mao as he stood up. The sky lay long on the horizon above the branches of the night forest.

"I'm going to see the executioner."

"I'm going too," said Yumi.

They set sail with ninety-nine aboard
Only one survived
And one bottle of rum

In high spirits, the executioner sang in a hoarse voice. Dawn was not far off.

"What was that youngster talking about—I have no intention of giving up this flame." He waved off Mao and Yumi's pleas and headed the swaying horse drawn cart back the way he had come. He was quite drunk, delighted at the prospect of making a profit on the deal. The flame burned in a hanging lamp on the horse cart.

"What are we going to do?" said Yumi anxiously looking up into Mao's face.

I see now—what I want for the townspeople probably can't come true. But, I must battle the executioner to beg the question of the infinite innocence which flows through the fowl in the sky and the townspeople as well. Mao raised his hand. A bevy of birds gathered round.

Bird wings came down with great force over the lamp which held the flame, nearly extinguishing it. Alarmed, the executioner moved the lamp to the other side of the cart.

"Whoa. You won't get away with this."

The next bird descended and as the flame was about to falter, the executioner spilled just a bit of the flame into the oil on the horse cart.

"I can't let the flame fail." I won't make a cent on this deal if the fire goes out, he thought.

Before his very eyes, the flame burned stronger, and the executioner, in the burning cart, sang louder and louder.

> They set sail with ninety-nine aboard
> Only one survived
> And one bottle of rum

The flames burned up into the sky and the entire flock of birds, one after another, fell from the sky, scorched.

The pheasant never returned, nor the owl nor the eagle. All the birds went up in flames and fell to earth.

Mao watched the burning cart with feelings of frustration and bitterness, and then suddenly raised both hands. He closed his eyes, and the elm leaves were suddenly below him as the sky lifted his wings. Mao, now a bird, flew off to put out the fire. He would do it for Yumi's sake.

"This damn bird won't quit." The executioner tried to wave off the bird that came at him in the burning cart. I can't turn a profit if I don't have any embers left.

The bird threw himself brutally at the flame. It was nearly dawn in the forest. The bird continued to make forays into the flames beating it with his wings and attacking the cart, shrieking all the while, "This is not a true flame!" The executioner ducked for cover as he watched the bird. And through all this the horse cart rolled forward still in flames.

The town welcomed the cart joyfully, and in no time fire was passed into the hands of the villagers. The executioner and the black swallowtail were greeted with roars of banzai!

Now that fire had been returned to the town, the flint stones were no longer any use. They became the blacksmith's tools. The volcano once again emitted sleepy wafts of smoke.

Along the forest path, Yumi picked up one red rose. She leaned over the burned body of the dead Mao, placed the rose on him and kissed his hair gently.

"Alas, my true flame is extinguished."

Hide-and-Not-Go-Seek

Hide-and-seek is a lonesome game. You hide in the dark barn redolent with straw and, holding very still, you feel the day coming to an end while waiting for the seeker to come.

You don't want to come out too soon thinking the game is over and suddenly be found, so you stay in hiding. The longer you hide the more you lose track of time. Sometimes you have only been hiding for five minutes, but it feels more like a year; or two hours can feel like five minutes.

Perhaps you worry that the seeker might not come to find you, and that you will have to stay hidden in the darkness of this barn for years; and you are overcome by a fulminating feeling that something terrible will happen. And if by chance you fall asleep hidden among the straw bundles, your anxiety only intensifies.

The barn door opens and in comes a man. He says, "Found you!", but his voice is strangely hoarse. When you step out, the seeker has already turned into an adult. He wears a gray suit and is attended by a young woman. The young woman is holding a baby and is smiling happily.

Without any reference to the twenty years that have passed, he says, "I looked for you for such a long time."

But there is no way you could know how long he has really been seeking you.

Yet, when you emerge from the barn the scenery has

changed completely, and all your playmates have grown to adulthood. It is terrifying to think that even though the entire world has grown older, the hider alone has not aged in the least. The hider loyally waits for the designated seeker. Hide-and-seek is such a heart-breaking game.

Every time I played hide-and-seek when I was a child, I was "it" because I could never win at rock-paper-scissors. It was not an easy task to find all the children successfully so the next child would take over the role of seeker, especially because there were the ones I didn't know from other neighborhoods. There were some bad apples in the bunch as well who would hide in manholes or in the attic of some random house, so I didn't have a prayer of finding them.

One day, I thought I would fix them by renouncing my role as seeker and going straight home without looking for them. You guys can just hide until you rot. I take no responsibility for the world moving on without you while you are still hiding, I thought to myself.

All this was well and good, but even though I wasn't keeping an eye on the hiders, they were keeping an eye on me, so my prank had virtually no effect. I was home playing the harmonica when the hiders showed up under my window shouting repeatedly, "We're ready! We're ready!" In the end, they broadcast their vitriol around the neighborhood yelling, "Hey, Seeker! Come out or else!"

The following day and the day after that, I was "it." I looked out as dusk descended over the knotweed and called weakly, "Are you ready?" and went off to seek that unruly gang. Those kids sure were good at hide-and-seek.

There was one freckle-faced kid in particular (who bore an

uncanny resemblance to me) who was sneaky and refused to come out until I gave up. I hated that kid.

Then one day as I was standing by a telephone pole calling, "Are you ready?" it suddenly occurred to me to peek and see where this kid went to hide. "I'm going to find him right off the bat and make him be 'it'."

I peeked through my fingers and saw all the kids disperse. Some went to the wheat field, some went behind the storage shed at my house, and that kid opened the manhole behind the shed. Even before I heard them call, "We're ready", I was after him like a shot circling to the rear of the shed.

The last I saw of that freckle-faced kid was his hand trying to close the manhole cover behind him. When the cover was back in place, the alleyway fell silent again and not a soul was in sight. In the late afternoon, only my long shadow lay across the manhole cover.

(This was not an ordinary manhole. It was a place for storing oil. It was about seven feet by seven feet of darkness which our family was not using at the time. It had been constructed for holding oil reserves during the winter.)

I was about to lift the lid and pronounce, "Found you!", but I thought better of it. A lumber truck had just come rumbling along. It was backing down our alley to drop off lumber right next to the storage shed for an addition to our chicken coop. "Off load the lumber right here," I called to the driver as I pointed to the manhole. "Got it!" the driver called back blithely and started to stack the lumber on the manhole cover. It must have been a mountain of lumber weighing over twelve hundred pounds. And because this reservoir was not used on a regular basis, I didn't "know" anything about someone hiding in it.

Finally, the truck took off and the manhole was sealed shut. I went to find the other hiders in the wheat field and yelled, "Found you!" with unsupressed delight.

The next day, however, there was no article in the newspaper about a child gone missing. I asked my hide-and-seek buddies about the freckle-faced kid, but nobody seemed to know which family he belonged to. This kind of thing was not infrequent, so no one gave it a second thought when the freckle-faced kid (who looked so much like me) didn't come out to play with us anymore. The following day, I went to the storage shed by myself. The warm sun shone down on the lumber stacked up high.

"I wonder if he's dead?" I thought to myself. I suddenly thought of the terrible thing I had done, but I knew there was absolutely no way I could move all that lumber myself, so I decided to keep quiet about the whole thing.

From that day on, I quit playing hide-and-seek. (I knew I would never be free of being the seeker until I found that freckle-faced kid.)

Fifteen years passed. I finished college, got a job in the city, and was working as a company man. One New Year's I decided to make a long-postponed visit to my hometown. I admired the wheat fields as green as ever. Feeling relaxed I played the beat-up old harmonica (the one I had as a kid) and was filled with a deep sense of nostalgia.

I shed my overcoat and told my mother I was going to stretch my legs. She sent me off saying, "Go ahead and have a nice walk around the old neighborhood." I slipped on a pair of sandals, went out into the garden and breathed in the fragrance of the pheasant's eye flower. But the instant I rounded the corner of the storage shed I remembered the hide-and-seek incident. What had happened to that child who resembled me so closely?

The lumber was no longer on top of the manhole. Other than some wilted dandelions clinging to the edge of the manhole cover, nothing had changed from fifteen years ago. I lifted the cover to find pitch blackness inside. A winter moth fluttered into the dark hole, and I slipped in as well, then lit a match. I crouched down wondering if the kid's bones were still here. The chill of the air hit me like a slap in the face. I went further into the hole, but as I tried to light another match I thought I heard someone pushing the manhole cover back into place. Startled, I looked up and caught a glimpse of the freckle- faced kid (as he was fifteen years ago) standing on the surface bathed in sunlight. I wanted to shout, "Open up!" but in my state of astonishment nothing came out. Then I heard it: bang, thud. It was the sound of something heavy being stacked on top of the lid. Then, I suddenly knew: it was the sound of lumber. (I knew I couldn't get the cover off by myself.) From above, I heard that kid call to the other hiders, "Are you ready?" It was a clear, beautiful voice, and I had a desperate feeling that I knew it from somewhere.

"Are you ready? Are you ready?"

Then I figured it out. It was none other than my own voice. That kid had become me and was about to go off and find the other kids as if he were "it." He was going to go home to my house at day's end. The lights would be on in that house and miso soup would be on the stove.

LENA'S DEATH

In the summer of that year, I learned the pleasures of smoking. And, without being aware of it, I also came to believe deeply in the bewildering law which states that all beings who do not forget become swans.

The first person I met was a sailor. He was a black man, born in San Domingo, and he bent down to join me in picking up the shells I had spilled on the stone stairs.

"What? Did you say the ocean?" I asked him back. I was on my way back home from the *lycée*.[1]

Upon closer inspection, I saw this black sailor was profoundly sad. This was adequately explained by his big ears alone. He said he was new to this town. Then he added in a gravelly, hesitant voice, "I want to sell a peacock. Do you know anyone who might be interested?"

I noticed that this country bumpkin's suitcase was covered with stickers from places like Santa Ana and Mont Parnasse. I immediately decided to trust him.

The coffee shop with the parrot was called The Yellow Wink. As soon as I pushed open the door, two young people who had apparently be kissing pulled apart. It made me wonder what kind of deserted dump the place was.

The bartender wrote the number "1" in on the blank calendar. In this town, the "first" was the first day you

1. French secondary school.

encountered someone. The parrot, in a good mood, screeched loudly.

"I have a peacock in my suitcase," said the black man.

"You have to show it to me," I said sipping my Manhattan, catching a whiff of a deal. "Peacocks don't like roofs or windows, you know."

"Well, where will you show it to me?"

"Down by the shore."

The desolate noon dunes immediately made a sundial of our two shadows. The black man walked behind me. This tall beanpole of a man had been silent.

"I guess this will do as well as anywhere."

"Fine."

The intense sunrays generated steam from the black man's large body. I took his suitcase in hand. Suddenly he shouted, "If you don't do what I tell you, I'll kill you."

I had been duped. I looked at him and saw the nearly concealed pistol in the black sailor's hand.

"Open the suitcase," he ordered. I already knew by this point that I shouldn't have been expecting a peacock. With fear and trepidation, I opened the suitcase. First, a pair of red shoes appeared, then feet and then the folded form of a sleeping dancer.

I closed my eyes. She's alive. Without giving it another thought, I knew I had no choice but to believe in the blue horizon just behind me. When I opened my eyes, still there was the prostrate dancer.

The black man tossed over a jackknife, and said, "Lena is my wife, but the bitch hid the fact that she was in love with Jean[2] the poet."

---

2. "Zhahn," as pronounced in French.

I looked into his face and saw that he was weeping tears of glass. A single parrot flew over and perched on the lid of the suitcase.

"She was transfused with memories from the poet Jean, and little by little as they accumulated, wings began to sprout from her back. I just couldn't bear to see her change into some bird creature."

"A bird?" I repeated.

"Yes. People who don't lose their memories turn into swans." The parrot piped up and repeated, "People who don't lose their memories turn into swans."

"But I can't kill Lena. I can't bear to see her go to Jean or be turned into a bird, either. I love her and that's why I have to make you kill her now."

"I am going to make you kill her." The parrot repeated the sailor's words, turning its back to the ocean.

"Stab her with this jackknife, or else I'll kill you." Blackie cocked the pistol. Startled by the sound, the parrot flew off in a flurry.

I picked up the jackknife and considered what to do. I don't want to die; and really, it would give me the pleasure of stabbing her beautiful breast, like pinning a specimen to a wall with the pin of happiness. Blackie the sailor urged me on.

"Come on, quick!"

I leaned forward and stabbed with the jackknife.

Bang! It was the sound of the pistol. As soon as I stabbed Lena, I was shot. All of a sudden, all that came into my field of vision was the dune. It was hot.

"Lena! Now you are finally mine!"

Blackie leapt over my inert body and hurried to the dead body of the dancer. He rocked her and wept bitterly.

"Lena, wings are already growing out of your back. You have already been contaminated with Jean's blood. Lena! You're really dead. You're dead. I have made a terrible mistake!"

He sat on the dune cross-legged and then he spoke. He put the pistol to his ear, the ear which looked like a pink whirlpool, a genetic trait in his ancestry.

"I will die with Lena. I will die with Lena. I will die with Lena."

I awoke to that repetition which sounded like the monotonous roar of the ocean. And then I realized that I was not going to rest in peace, despite the fact that I died alongside someone killed in passion.

Night had fallen. Blackie was dead, still sitting cross-legged. I clasped my hands together and realized that I had to give the prostrate Lena's beauty a sea burial.

A sea burial is a simple affair. I folded her up once again, packed her in the suitcase, then stood on the dune holding the *lycée* hat with the feather. I hurled the suitcase into the sea. It capsized once and then bobbed up.

I decided to go home. It was at that moment when I realized that nothing had happened to me.

* * * * *

There were two people everyone knew who lived on either side of the river which cut through the town. The pallid wife set the one-eyed crow atop the record of "The Falling Baron" overture and listened as it spun. Rumor had it that this married woman absconded with stars from the sky every night. Consequently, every day the number of girls who went blind in the town increased. It was astonishing that she was the sole possessor of blond hair, yet she had no emotional attachment to it and was perfectly able to experience pleasure even without the benefit of that hair color.

This woman owned a hand mirror. Whomever she loved would appear in the mirror whenever she desired. She could be in the comfort of her bed and be able to caress anyone she thought of. It was in this way that the poor poet Jean, who lived on the other side of the river, was gradually overtaken by this woman, without even being aware of it.

"Louis!" The woman called the crow.

"*Oui*," answered the crow as he spun atop the LP. "How Quiet it is Tonight."

Perhaps for the same reason bundles of bills flowed into the pockets of the invincible Baron Fan-Fan La Dali, oceans flowed into this town's black, muddy river.

By the time Lena, the swan, drifted under the bridge, Jean the poet, who lived in an attic, had reached the extremes of poverty. He had spent the last two nights writing nothing but poems about his amorous feelings for Lena the Dancer. So overcome was he that he even called out her name.

It was already late into the night when the silence summoned the woman's desire. "My dear, Louis . . ." she said with a tormented air as she, pale as ever, released the crow. The crow flew up tearing off the pale woman's dress with its beak. She, now sleekly disrobed, got into bed her long hair trailing across the floor. She took up her mirror.

The swan is a bird which has forgotten how to forget. Lena the swan recalled Jean the poet painfully as she floated along with the current. Dear Jean, you support my new wings

119

with the blood of a poet. Though she did not have human words, she attempted to call for Jean the poet.

Jean attributed his inability to conjure up a visual image in his head to the heat. He opened the window to see the river in the darkness below. All of a sudden he whispered, "What's this? Something odd is floating this way."

The woman was astonished. What could be happening? The mirror reflected nothing tonight, of all nights. She looked, crazed, into the mirror. Then a most unexpected voice came from her bed.

"Jean, where are you?"

These were the first words Lena spoke as a swan. "Jean, where are you?"

Time after time Lena the swan cried out painfully.

Jean dashed out and saw a single white swan. As he took the bird in his arms and lifted it up, the poet wondered if the mute swan were trying in vain to speak. The red shoes were not at all wet, so he thought that perhaps it was a messenger from Lena, but that might have been the poet's imagination.

"It's you. Jean, it's really you."

With the violent sound of wings, a young girl appeared in the woman's mirror. It was the figure of Lena the Dancer before she became a swan. She approached affectionately, "Jean, blood of the poet, I was killed at sea. I am now a swan."

"But it's really me—Lena! Don't you recognize these red shoes?"

"Those gestures remind me of my love who is far away, but this is a bird . . ." he half murmured.

"I'm not a bird. It's me—Lena. Have you forgotten my red shoes? You took them off my feet at my boarding house on your way home from the racetrack. Have you already forgotten those red shoes?"

The woman could no longer bear the voice from within the mirror. She covered the girl in the mirror with both hands, but as she did, her hands sunk straight into the mirror itself. The woman put her hands on Lena's face and pushed with all her might. With that, the woman fell farther into mirror, her whole body pitching forward. The naked body of that woman went sprawling rapidly into the depths of the night, her blond hair streaming after her into the darkness.

"Jean, won't you remember?" It was only that voice which remained. The crow, Louis, simply repeated *oui* timorously, over and over. Louis had only been taught one word and that was *oui*. "*Oui, oui.*"

"The mother swan and the signet are weeping." Jean stared at the swan intensely.

"I am sorry to have interrupted your journey." Jean released the swan from the bridge. Once again, the swan had no choice but to follow the current of the ever-flowing river into the night.

The swan grew smaller in the distance. "There might be a letter from Lena", said Jean the poet, who at length began to walk silently back the way he had come.

"Why did you let me go, Jean? I'm floating farther and father away from you. Jean! Jean!"

The crow, head cocked to one side, resolutely repeated *oui* time and again before the mirror.

Fallen Angel

The town was thrown into a deranged state of confusion at the very hint of Don's return. The Casket, a basement bar, gloomily closed its doors in the morning, and the half blind stray dog eyed a piece of newspaper blown about with palpable anxiety. Everyone in town turned pale. The only thing that looked fresh was the cabbage at the market.

But the returning Don, referred to derisively as Blackie, had lost his memory. He had come back with nothing more than his signature wan smile. The white felt fedora suited him oddly enough, but perhaps that was because it was July. Even the parrot perched on his shoulder continuously berated him with "*Tu te moques*."[1] The barber, who grew cactus, said "You see, he was K.O.-ed in a fight in San Domingo."

There were two people in town who did not believe Don had lost his memory: the elementary school teacher and the clothier. The old spinster teacher, Miss Kate, said in her piercing voice, "He never had a memory to begin with." Her narrowed eyes darted furtively at the grape leaves.

Yet, it was actually the clothier who was particularly surprised and then saddened. In his timid and faint-hearted way, it was his custom to rise early and hurriedly read the newspaper cover to cover and declare, when he had finally

---

1. Loser!

assured himself that a report of his death had not appeared, with a heavy sigh of relief, "I'm still alive!"

So, when he learned of Don's return, he jumped to the conclusion that Don had, no doubt, come back to take revenge on him. He was convinced of this because he had made a pinstripe waistcoat for him when Don was at the height of his talents as a boxer. He had shrewdly scrimped on one button to increase his profit margin, and considered this thrilling moment of exploiting the hooligan a lifelong accomplishment worthy of commemoration.

All the town clocks sung this refrain: *Il arriva un malheur!* [2]

"The day of misfortune has come," people thought as they puffed on cigarettes. In this town, depending on the circumstances, misfortune was, on occasion, welcomed happily as a measure of their good fortune.

Don was walking along the riverside and heard the bell in the clock tower. His countenance clouded like an overcast sky, despite the roses blossoming everywhere and the popularity of the traveling theater troupe.

Truth be told, Don was in love. He was in love with the girl who sold flowers. Then and now, she sells roses at the entrance to the bar The Whimsical Star across the street from the racetrack. Strangely enough, no one had ever heard her speak. Yet, it wasn't that she couldn't speak. Rumor had it that perhaps she was only able to speak when in the presence of one she loved. And that was precisely how it was.

A pale man played the part of Romeo in the traveling theater troupe. He was universally panned in that role. Most people thought that this Romeo apparently had no perceptive abilities whatsoever, barely opening his mouth, eyes damp. In

2. The day of misfortune has come.

mid-performance, he would falter, unable to say the line to his Juliet, "My sweet love . . ."; or he would say "go away" when he should have said "come hither," or say, "I hate you" when he should have said "I love you." He was stunningly handsome like Jean-Louis Barrault[3] in his younger years, and his acting was brimming with sadness enough to forget even forgetting.

It was a morning when the brilliance of green foliage stings the eye. Don, somehow now in a good mood, purchased a suitcase. The town went into a frenzy that day. The flower girl had disappeared. The bar owner of The Casket, very agitated, smashed a glass.

"Politics is to blame for this!" But, it was really Don who abducted her. He carefully folded her up, packed her into the suitcase and was gone in the blink of an eye.

At the racetrack a black thoroughbred galloped in a race already underway. The crowd roared. Don never looked back.

Don and the parrot stayed put in his lodgings until evening. Then when he opened the suitcase, roses spilled out. Blackie was excited, but the flower girl had stiffened and remained motionless and unconscious. It was almost as if she had lost all color like a pallid doll. He and the parrot considered what to do.

The pale young man, exhausted, left the theater after his performance was over. The young woman who played Juliet whispered after him, "How could you? How could you?" Eyes brimming with tears, and an expression of unexplained jealousy, she resentfully threw a fan, redolent with flame, into the night. Suddenly a moth fell.

---

3. Jean-Louis Barrault (1910–1994), a French actor, director, and mime.

Juliet sat alone, eyes downcast, at the table set for two. "There's nothing for it." It's not just the theater; he doesn't want to live with me anymore, either.

Presently, the pale young man waded into the river and floated along on his back, for love resides where a river flows.

Suddenly, it came to Don. All he had to do was find something stronger than love to restore the flower girl to consciousness. At which point the parrot screamed, "Fire!" That was it. It had to be fire. Blackie Don took from his pocket matches from The Casket and struck one. A single star appeared outside the window when he did.

The young man floated as far as the bamboo rushes on the riverbank and then climbed ashore. And there stood the ruins of an ancient gambling hall. The outdoor lights had failed now, and thus it was pitch dark.

Don pushed the door open with a creak. The hallway before him was strewn thickly with playing cards. He went down the hall and was about to enter the room at the end, but when he struck a match on the flower girl's shoe, she said, "Wait."

Far away, the pale man suddenly stood stock-still. Don, taken aback, put out the match and kissed the flower girl ardently. Yet, the kiss felt as dry as paper. Don struck another match. Again one more star appeared. The flame made a crackling sound as it burned the flower girl's feet. In this concrete room, the parrot cocked its head and dredged up words in its own mind.

This time, it was the pale man who entered the room. As always, he faced the darkness and said, "Today's the day when I will say my name." The darkness responded, "Say nothing."

The pale man spoke as if trying to catch the darkness before it got away, "Just one thing—I loved you."

"If you loved me, then what's in a name?"

"What do you mean what's in a name?! See! I am Blackie Don, the Boxer!"

Don responded to the flower girl's words, wild with joy. But the flower girl seemed not to hear him. This was because her words were meant for the pale man. The flower girl continued to burn even more intensely, like a doll on fire.

"Our troupe leaves today, but Romeo does not bid you farewell."

"Romeo does not bid you farewell," squawked the parrot. Don, however, was not listening. Tears welled up in his eyes. He showered kisses on the burning flower girl, on her hair, her cheek, her flames. Yet, when the flames finally died down there was nothing left but one sheet of newspaper.

Stars invite bitter winter winds, but it was still November. Don wept. And while he wept, gradually something was rekindled inside him by this lost love restoring memories of things past: the boxing ring, roses, the San Domingo match, how he was tortured when he didn't make good on throwing a fight, the sea's melancholy, his mother's necklace, the letter riddled with lies.

I was young. The fancy dress ball, the applause—Where am I? What is this newspaper here for? He picked it up and there was a picture of the woman from Monte Carlo standing next to the one-eyed black horse who had won at the track. After his crying jag, he wandered out for a drink. Maybe I should raise a little hell. The parrot remained behind. "Romeo does not bid you farewell."

The pale man saw one long stemmed rose at his feet as

he made his way home. He picked it up and breathed in its gentle scent. He couldn't place the fragrance, and without bothering to give it any more thought, he tossed the rose aside. Behind him stretched a long hallway.

About the Author and the Translator

Terayama Shūji (1935–1983) was one of the most prolific "outlaw" writers in the 1960s and 70s in Japan. He produced an enormous body of work in multiple genres ranging from poetry, essays, novels, short stories, film scripts and plays. His work was often of a provocative nature, and thus he was branded as an iconoclast and agitator, frequently relegated to the fringes of even those among the literati expressing counterculture, revolutionary ideas about social behavior, sexuality and philosophy.

Elizabeth L. Armstrong has been teaching Japanese language at Bucknell University since 1999. She has also worked as an interpreter/translator both in Japan and the United States. This is her first published translation.